JONAH CAMPBELL

EATEN BACK TO LIFE

(ESSAYS)

JONAH CAMPBELL

EATEN BACK TO LIFE
(ESSAYS)

Invisible Publishing
Halifax & Picton

Library and Archives Canada Cataloguing in Publication

Campbell, Jonah, 1981-, author
    Eaten back to life / Jonah Campbell.

Issued in print and electronic formats.
ISBN 978-1-926743-92-9 (softcover).--ISBN 978-1-926743-97-4 (EPUB)

    1. Gastronomy. 2. Food. 3. Food--Humor. 4. Campbell, Jonah, 1981-.
I. Title.

TX631.C358 2017   641.01'3   C2017-903078-7
                                                 C2017-903079-5

Edited by John Semley
Cover and interior design by Megan Fildes | Typeset in Laurentian
With thanks to type designer Rod McDonald

Printed and bound in Canada

Invisible Publishing | Halifax & Picton
www.invisiblepublishing.com

We acknowledge the support of the Canada Council for the Arts, which last year invested $20.1 million in writing and publishing throughout Canada.

 Canada Council   Conseil des Arts
for the Arts   du Canada

For Barbara, still

"I'd trade it all for a little more."
—C. Montgomery Burns

Introduction

I have known Jonah Campbell for a handful of years by now—a decade and change, by my count. Which I suppose constitutes two handfuls. And change. In that time I have seen him howl mad at a Morrissey concert; watched him stab open a can of garbage National Bohemian Beer with a knife produced seemingly from nowhere; I have attempted to radiate annoyance while he talked in depth with an obliging Parisian sommelier about the provenance of certain grapes and the repute of this-or-that vintner and god-only-knows-what-else, but nevertheless given myself over to his (allegedly) better judgment; I have heroically held my tongue while he dozed hungover in the back seat of an acquaintance's grandmother's car with his face almost totally obscured by one of those quilted sleeping masks worn in old movies by the kinds of characters who also own monogrammed robes; laughed when he left me a rambling phone message after failing to keep our appointment at his old Saint-Henri apartment (christened "Snake Hollow") that involved the presumably explanatory/excusatory declaration, "shit got baffled"; and watched with perverse amusement, as he registered seemingly unaffected indifference to the sight of the *Mona Lisa*, widely considered one of the better paintings ever painted.

But the best and most telling story, the one that winds to the heart of the particular quality of Jonah-ness that defines his character and, so too, this collection, came to me secondhand. It runs as follows: in an effort to get the better of the suffocating summertime heat, he and some mutual friends went swimming somewhere—a lake or a quarry or one of those ol' swimmin' holes you hear about, it doesn't really matter. But, like, not a pool. Anyway. When a friend commented on how great the water was and what a capital idea going swimming on a hot day turned out to be, Jonah replied, in an archly Jonah-ish turn (voice lilting upward in my mind, if not in reality): "It's almost...too refreshing?" At which point our mutual friend, consumed by exasperated disgust, attempted to angrily, impotently paddle away in an inner tube.

The author (of this collection; not your present author, i.e., me) has debated the finer points of this story, but that it lives as such in legend is just as well. And also sort of the point. The idea of a heat-beating dip proving, somehow, too refreshing seems categorically contradictory. How, after all, can something be in excess of refreshment? Isn't there refreshment, and that's it? Presumably, if something is either a) exceedingly refreshing, or b) insufficiently refreshing, it thus ceases to be at all refreshing, and so the modifier essentially slaughters the thing it's modifying. Simply: it doesn't make sense.

And yet, I think this anecdote reveals a certain quality in Jonah's writing, and in his thinking (if it is not too pretentious or haughty to call it that). Throughout this collection, which spans everything from the serious consideration of emerging chip flavours to a defence of dilettantism to canny observations on the films of Jean Renoir, Jonah's work is structured around a sustained discontent. He holds in his mind—or even, I'll dare to venture, sappily, his heart—ideas of things that just exceed (or far exceed) the cold, boring reality of things themselves. It's too easy to get locked the cliché of "Platonic ideals" and whatnot, but suffice it to say that for Jonah there always seems to be this imagined essence of an experience or thing toward which his work inevitably narrows: the geographic and historic particularity of the profile of a particularly funky (in the gross, noxious sense, not the slinky bass-solo sense) glass of wine, or of his encounter with that wine, the concentrations of flavours found in bitters and digestifs, even the essential character of what a place, or holiday, or piece of candy, or potato chip means. This preoccupation, perhaps in its very nature, creates conditions that can never be fully realized. It can only be perceived in flashes, like the face of a hot babe glimpsed speeding by on a train.

There's an overriding disappointment in this. If there's one thing that draws me to Jonah's writing on food, boozing, and whatever else, it's the mood of melancholy that governs the proceedings (I'm also undeniably suckered in by his acute eye for detail and capacity to turn a phrase, and his penchant for crapulence, which I share, albeit in a way that's less refined and more just run-of-the-mill-fat-guy). Jonah's writing is shot through with a sense of dissatisfaction, yet it is, I think, a productive dissatisfaction.

This is not because such feelings of always being let down carry with them some cheesy hope of one day, somehow, somewhere, finding that perfect sandwich, like: *Lo, that one day we may be able to eat kebab unburdened by the guilt of colonialism!* God, no. Garish! What I respond to in Jonah's disappointment is the intensity with which it complicates pleasure. In his best pieces, he approaches the fineries of life—and the not-so-fineries, like getting shitcanned in Niagara Falls, Ontario, a place where I too have spent many bleary nights shambling recklessly under the ambivalent glare of a three-story sculpture of Frankenstein holding a Whopper—with caution, even disdain. Pleasure is supposed to be the thing we escape into, to relieve ourselves from the weary realities of the world. And yet it's in this escape itself that Jonah seems to find (or create) the weariest problem: the vexing contradictions at the heart of being alive and eating and drinking and losing ourselves to the delusive succour of—to yoink a favourite Kramerism—feeling good all the time. He leaves the problem of squaring the accoutrements of "the good life" with actually living a good, morally unsuspect life unsolved, as it should be.

It comes back to that idea of excess, itself a governing force in the modern Western world. Perhaps we can only mull over the conditions of such gross excess after subjecting ourselves to the full gauntlet of its abuses. It's not about drinking so much and then being punished with a hangover. It's about drinking so much to get hungover, suffering the punishment like a wretch and then, slowly, eating ourselves back to life. It's about the bracing reality that to be refreshed at all is to feel too refreshed.

And so: here's to feeling bad all the time.

—John Semley

---

1 Though Mr. Campbell assures me that it was not a proper sleeping mask but rather a T-shirt wrapped around his face, to achieve the general effect of a sleeping mask.

A Note on the Definitions

Unless otherwise specified, all etymologies and definitions are drawn from *The Compact Oxford English Dictionary*, 1971. The choice is part affectation, part affection, as the author wishes to preserve some of the historical artifactuality of the language, and also likes the heft of the thing itself. Conversely, for spelling, italicization and usage, we have attempted to adhere as much as possible to the *Canadian Oxford Dictionary*, except where the author attempts to make "a big deal" out of it (see "Postscript: On Italicization").

A Bag of Assholes

Paris in the summertime is a strange place. Summer is, as anyone could tell you, the worst time to visit, as half of the restaurants are closed, all of the Parisians are on vacation, and in their stead are masses of gaping tourists from the likes of which the rest of us take great pains and great pride to distinguish ourselves, in spite of the fact that the Parisians hate us all more or less equally. But we all make poor decisions now and then, so once I went to Paris in July and dutifully discovered that it was too hot to eat and no one has air conditioning and my grand plans of plumbing the depths of French food and wine had to be subordinated to the more immediate necessity of using an infinity of miniature Kronenbourgs to keep from expiring in a sopping pile on the floor. There were a few moments of reprieve, of course— goose rillettes with white Irouléguy from a spot I persist in misremembering as the "Cave of the Abyss," the first and best *mimolette* I have ever had (a cheese temporarily banned in the United States for, as a rule, containing mites), and as much and as varied kebab as I could get into me.

But my most successful, or least most instructive, outing was to a little *cave à manger* in the 9e arrondissement that had been favourably reviewed and distinguished from another establishment's "comically pretentious team of radish-fetish nitwits"[1] by its execution of traditional, unfussy French fare. I rolled by on a comparatively temperate Wednesday afternoon and found the place quite deserted. The *cave à manger*, it should be noted, is not so much a restaurant as it is a wine shop that has a couple of tables, a short food menu, and considerably lower markups on bottles than one encounters in a restaurant. The term has become much abused in Paris, but generally one can expect an operation that falls somewhere between a wine shop and a bistro. I ordered a glass of some spritzy Loire red about which I remember very little, and, from the handful of dishes chalked up on the board at the end of the room, I opted for the *andouillette*.

I considered opening this account with the line "This summer in France, I was defeated by a sausage." Let me just say that I did have some idea, when ordering, what I was in for. I know what *andouillette* is. I know what *andouillette* is made of, and didn't really *think* I would like it. *Larousse Gastronomique* describes it as "a type of sausage made from pork intestines (*chaudins*), often with the addition of pork stomach and calf's mesentery, precooked in stock or milk and packed into a skin." What this already evocative description leaves out is the extent to which andouillette is defined by the use of lower intestine, and consequently the extent to which it smells like actual shit garbage on account of it being, yes, basically just a cooked bag of assholes. This is for what *andouillette* is known, loved, and maligned by diverse parties. It is pungent and aggressive and all up in one's face, and I, for all that I am drawn to things that taste bad and gross and great (bretty beers, oxidative sherries, bitters of all kinds—all booze, it occurs to me), I am nonetheless not a great fan of powerfully funky charcuterie, or the more "organy" and elect of the offal family.

Hence there was truly no reason for me to expect to like the *andouillette*. However, I had heard good things about the dish at this particular establishment—that it was rustic and expressive and *fidèle* (whether to Lyon or Troyes or wherever, or to some Platonic ideal, I don't know), so in spite of my trepidation and reasonable prediction that it would not be to my tastes, I was curious. And when better to try the thing than when faced with a specimen of agreed-upon quality? I was in France, for god's sake. I hadn't come for the watery beer and state racism alone, that's for sure.

And I couldn't hack it. Oh boy, could I not hack it. I mean, I tried, in what fashion passes for "valiantly" in the wasteland of moral fibre that is my interior mental landscape. Which is to say that having ordered it I had to *try* to eat it, even though upon splitting the casing of the quite substantial sausage I was treated to the rather robust aroma for which *andouillette* is so prized. Which is butts. Butts, unmistakably. But like, living butts, if that means anything. Not shit per se, but like a butt that you are nonetheless fully occupied with. And so, taking grateful advantage of the almost equally pungent (oh, if only it had been more pungent still) mustard with which the sausage was served, I consumed something like one-third (I would flatter myself to say a full half) of the generously provided length. Then, as befitting any self-respecting gastronome, I feigned getting an important phone call and asked for the remains to be wrapped up to go. For this is what "pride" means, in the life that I apparently have made for myself: sitting alone at a table in a casual wine-shop-cum-resto in Paris, France, pantomiming a non-existent phone conversation for the sake of the no-one-at-all who is in the room with me, on the off chance that the peripheral vision of the chef or proprietor is sufficiently acute to register my bland Canadian embarrassment at not being unable to appreciate this sausage that so notoriously tastes like butts.

Not, for the record, that it tasted *bad*, for it actually tasted very good, but it tasted like something good that had also been in, or was, a butt. Like, a pig's butt, I guess. Delicious and disgusting simultaneously. Pleasure and repulsion wrenched from their zero-sum relationship through uneasy liaison. In that respect, I am sure it was an exemplary and well-crafted *andouillette*. This is what it's like to be defeated by a sausage.

But it's not defeat, truly, because as vulnerable as is my account to this interpretation, eating the sausage was not about proving something. It was not about triumphing over the food. It was, and is, above all about the attempt to make space for new pleasure in one's life, not only for one's own satisfaction, but as a gesture of faith in the possibility of intersubjective understanding: maybe based on what I know, I won't like this, I don't like this. But someone likes this, they know how to like this. It is not a competition, although it is a challenge; it is a call to understanding and to enjoyment both—*others love me*, the sausage cries, *why don't you?* One need not out of some abstract devotion to gastronomy love everything that is cool or weird or rarefied or rustic, of course, but there is something gross in the too-easy repair to the refuge of "personal taste." The irony of the adage that "there is no accounting for taste" is that while there are reams of sociological, anthropological, and historical writings accounting for taste in all sorts of ways, there forever remains an intimate kernel of indeterminacy, and one can never count on the socializing of tastes to be totalizing, complete. One could say that this kernel of indeterminacy is what makes taste insistently personal. The problem with the notion of the unassailable subjectivity of taste, however, is the presumption that the subject itself is stable and that desire and enjoyment are transparent. "I know what I like" is easy to affirm and impossible to argue against, but what happens when it turns out we are wrong? When it turns out we don't know what we like? What is the implication when the ultimate in subjective authority is (regularly, perhaps perpetually) eroded? It happens all the time. Or at least it could, if we let it.

It would be too strong to claim that one necessarily comes to understand others (or the Other) better by appreciating their culinary pleasures. This is a well-worn cliché of even the better food writing, and it veers too easily from empathy into appropriation, into the Eating of the Other. But there is certainly merit in trying to understand their appreciation, if only to destabilize the solipsism of pleasure, to undermine on a very intimate level the authority of the subject we assume defines the contours of our experience of the world. One never knows, but how often otherwise has one the opportunity to declare: if fate had it that I was to be defeated by a bag of assholes, I am happy it was thus?

---

1 From Aaron Ayscough's consistently worthy and enjoyable blog, *Not Drinking Poison in Paris*.

Apples, as Rain or Tears

I am infatuated with this Calvados. I want to hold a cup of it between fantastically callused hands as I wake up with the sun. I want to appreciate it in a yellow pavilion between rounds of Russian roulette with a jealous baron. I want to put too much of it away playing dice in the winter, drink it in my underwear while I look out the window waiting for summer to come. I want to and I will. The nights are getting warmer; it won't be long.

Because this drink does something that I love in wine, but which I don't often encounter in spirits. It seems to speak to a life that it had before it became a drink. Maybe not of a place in the sense of "terroir" per se, because if it speaks of a place I think it speaks of many places, but of a materiality prior to that artful abstraction that is potable alcohol (apologies for the alliteration). An earthiness, but also a worldliness, in the original sense of the word. For it tastes like apples. Apples in the world.

When one thinks of distilled spirits, one tends to imagine the essence of a thing, be it grain or grape or cane, shorn of its impurities and elevated, transformed. A pure expression. But a pure expression of what? It is difficult not to get entangled in metaphysical analogies, given the common vocabulary of spirits. In this case, however, the conventional (metaphysical) understanding of the spirit as *prior* to the flesh is confounded by a (alcoholic) spirit that tastes so distinctly of apples—not of some abstract or Platonic ideal of apples, but rather of apples of varying ripeness, the crisp and tart mingling with the already bruised and almost-rank-in-their-blunt-and-volatile-sweetness, apples that come from trees and hang on trees and eventually fall from trees, get kicked around in the dirt or covered with leaves or eaten by stupid pigs—that it can only be understood as a spirit *of* the flesh. Not a spirit that animates the world, but one that is animated *by* the world, an expression of all the impurities, failures, and accidents of life. Note that this is quite at odds with Cartesian or transcendentalist notions of body and spirit being of irreconcilable and fundamentally different stuff. The soul in this picture is not confined for a time to the living hell of materiality, but rather is forged in and of that flesh. Essence follows existence.

Likewise, this suggests a different reading of the idea of eau-de-vie, the French term for various brandies and fruit distillates, which literally translates as "water of life." Deriving from the Latin *aqua vitae*, and having its roots seemingly in Arabic scientific and alchemical investigation, eau-de-vie retains something of this transcendentalist gloss. To the extent that alcohol was viewed as a water of life, it was in a medical sense, as a life-giving elixir or purgative; or at points in the Middle Ages a metaphor for the purifying elixir of divinity. That which washes away the sins of the flesh. "My Soule had Caught an Ague," Edward Taylor cried, "and like Hell Her thirst did burn..."[1] But in this, my so-to-speak "immanentalist" approach, the water of life runs much more troubled and murky.

The cheap, precious aesthete in me hoped to find some greater insight by inquiring into the origins of the word *distillation*. However, all this yielded was a reminder of how reaching is my above metaphysical speculation. The "purification of essence" sense of the word seems to be of more recent vintage, rather than the root of its etymology. *Distill* refers, quite empirically, to the formation of drops; in fact, to the dropping or dripping of drops: *destillare*. *Stilla* = drop, the diminutive of *stiria*, for icicle (how cute). "To trickle down or fall in minute drops, as rain; tears," reads the *Oxford English Dictionary*.

And so, by speaking of distillates rather than spirits, we may be firmly back on materialist terrain, because yes, obviously alcoholic spirits are only metaphorically, not metaphysically, the souls of their source ingredients. I am not above using booze as a way of thinking through and around the materialist-transcendentalist divide, however. If the Calvados may be said to be a pure expression, not of a Platonic or *ur*-apple, but of a very worldly apple, so may I make use of these impressions to work toward some notion of essential qualities being not a priori, but contingent, accidental.

Anyway, it is good. I don't usually like saying that things taste like "late afternoon sun coming through the leaves," but there is some of that. It also tastes like autumn and hay and butterscotch. It tastes like what you needed all winter. Or I suppose to save time you could say "rustic, and a little funky." You know, like Levon Helm and the Band. But French.

---

1 Edward Taylor, "Meditation 10, Joh. 6.55. My Blood is Drinke indeed," quoted in "Edward Taylor and the Cleansing of 'Aqua Vitae,'" Kathy Siebel and Thomas M. Davis, *Early American Literature*, vol. 4, no. 3, 1969/1970.

Futures of Nostalgia, and
Other Thoughts on Places for Drinking

On another afternoon that summer in Paris, I found myself seeking sanctuary in Harry's New York Bar, just off the Avenue de l'Opéra. Famously the place of origin of the French 75 and the Bloody Mary, perhaps more famously patronized by Hemingway, the Fitzgeralds, Gertrude Stein, George Gershwin, et cetera. Reputedly the oldest cocktail bar in Paris, which confers a somewhat dubious honour given the nigh impossibility of finding a decent cocktail in the city,[1] in spite of the wealth of native vermouths and aperitifs (Byrrh, Bonal, Picon, Salers Gentiane, Dolin, and so on). Harry's is a beautiful bar, not quite like the gleaming French brasseries, but with a time-worn elegance that is restrained foremost by its need to remain legibly, unfussily "American."[2] As the story goes, what became Harry's New York Bar was literally a bar in New York City, chopped up, shipped overseas, and reconstructed in Paris in the early twentieth century to remedy what was even then perceived as a dearth of good places to have a bunch of boozes artfully splashed together into a single cup. It is clear that great pains were taken to produce the impression that not much has changed in the decor, comportment, menu, or philosophy. What was most impressive, however, was how quiet it was inside: a calm, cool quiet that went deeper than the lack of music, as if someone had cut a chunk out of the sticky, suffocating heat of the afternoon and slotted the building in its place. It was immeasurably restoring.

Harry's brings to mind another bar of historic note, an older bar in a younger city: McSorley's Old Ale House. In 1940 Joseph Mitchell wrote "The Old House at Home," a

Jonah Campbell

profile for the *New Yorker* of the bar, which is located just off
Third Avenue and East Seventh Street in Manhattan, where
the Bowery ended back when that really meant something.
Mitchell's claim that McSorley's was the oldest saloon
in the city (established in 1854) has been disputed, but it
was even then, before the U.S. had entered WWII, already
considered an anachronism, a dusty cave rich with Old New
York history. Arriving there myself seventy-two years later
(the bar now almost twice as old as it was when Mitchell
wrote of it), I am inclined to think it rich with the dust of
Old New York as well. The place is awesomely filthy. The
floor is covered in sawdust, there's a pot-bellied wood stove
in one corner that provides heat in the winter, several of
the tables are just old cable spools, and everything above
eye level is black with the kind of grimy dust that you can
tell feels tacky to the touch just by looking at it, that once
disturbed threatens to make you over in its own smudged
image. They serve only beer, "light" or "dark," in small
mugs, and always two at a time for some reason, two for
five dollars. The bartender has a tired-dad look about him
and walks with a heavy limp, spending what time he can
with his feet up on the bar. He tells me he's been tending
bar there for forty-five years, in addition to the two he spent
drinking at McSorley's before that. It is strange sitting in a
place that embodies so much of what the nouveau rustic of
contemporary design emulates, a place that is down to its
timbers just waiting to be "reclaimed" and put to aesthetic
work in some Prohibition-style "speakeasy" a block down
the street (McSorley's somehow weathered the Volstead
Act without closing or becoming a speakeasy).

It would be too easy and too trite to cast McSorley's as
merely a fading artifact of a more authentic past, although
it is that. For it is an artifact in a dual sense that draws on

both the archaeological and scientific meanings of the word. It is both a living relic of a bygone era and a living example of the drinking-hole-as-nostalgic-topos. Clearly, conscious decisions have been made to retain and amplify the shabby, old-fashioned charm of the place (short of hiring Ed Lauter to be the barman). The satisfaction to be derived from its authenticity is thus very much the product of a certain kind of nostalgia work. But, for all that artifactuality (I hesitate to say artificiality), these charms are no less real. When I first read "The Old House at Home," my desire to see McSorley's was tempered by the expectation that it would by now be thoroughly and obnoxiously commodified as a tourist experience, gleaming like a TGI Fridays in the night, selling history like hotcakes.[3] So I was pleasantly surprised to find a place so seemingly genuinely at ease with its dumpiness. Admittedly, I strolled in on a frigid Sunday night in February, but I like to think that the cheap beer, dinge, and liverwurst and onion sandwiches maintain a certain amount of this atmosphere at most hours (perhaps excepting the weekend, when I am given to understand it is wall-to-wall with tourists).

It has been claimed that George Gershwin composed *An American in Paris* in the piano bar downstairs at Harry's, and whether true or not, it is a fitting story. Not only because Harry's is quite literally, down to its struts and panelling, an American bar in Paris, but because Gershwin devised *An American in Paris* to chart a sort of impressionistic journey of an American expat dazzled by the sights and sounds of the city, momentary lapsing into a sort of nostalgic melancholy signified by a blues passage: "Our American friend, perhaps after strolling into a café and having a few drinks, has suddenly succumbed to a spasm of homesickness," read Gerswhin's notes.[4] I cannot speculate as to the feel of Harry's in the twenties, but it is in a sense originally nostalgic, a place constructed from the pieces of another place, at least spatially distant if not so removed in time, to be a haven and haunt (at least partly) for American tourists and expats. It is perhaps now doubly nostalgic, or characterized by a sort of second-order nostalgia, and Harry's wears it passably well, although with a little less easy confidence than McSorley's. McSorley's is still sprayed wall-to-wall (and floor-to-ceiling) with material Americana, but it comes across as patina rather than pastiche. Harry's New York Bar seems intentionally and very artificially frozen in time, trapped somewhere between dignity and Disneyland, whereas McSorley's feels more like it's suspended between the 1860s and an insurance fire.

All said, however, if both trade heavily in nostalgia, they do so earnestly and harmlessly—they have the pedigree of physically existing spaces that have been there, each for over a century, and so the slide from preservation into artifice is understandable, perhaps inevitable. They lie on the other end of the spectrum, perhaps on a different spectrum entirely, from something like, say, Bier Markt, the Ontario chain (a property of the same corporation that owns Swiss Chalet, New York Fries, and, most tellingly, East Side Mario's) that seems to be motivated by an attempt to combine a vague European beer-garden aesthetic with that of a Hooters. Bier Markt opened an outpost a few years ago in Montreal, and to their credit, they do have a lot of beer, much of which is international and in short supply in Quebec. I do not know if the Montreal iteration is on-message for the brand (I suspect yes), but the space is cavernous, two-tiered, and conspicuously gaudy, slick with the rapidly congealing afterbirth of a newly installed chain restaurant attempting to conjure the mythic grace of the—or perhaps any—"Old Country." Its brass and pounded tin cry out for the patina that they shall never be allowed to accrete, and so it is destined to reside in perpetuity (or until it folds in three years) as a European beer hall chez Disney, its looming Manneken Pis (the famous naked urinating toddler fountain sculpture of Belgium) mutely proclaiming its aridity by dint of the absence of anything to piss or anywhere in which to piss, save onto the arriving clientele or anyone else who happens to turn around and find themselves faced by the yawning urethras of any of the eight-foot fake stone babies that populate the building.

It is, I suppose, beyond nostalgia. Beyond history perhaps. Where we perceive a chain of events, the fibreglass Manneken Pis sees one single catastrophe that keeps piling wreckage upon wreckage and hurls it in front of his feet. The child would like to stay, awaken the dead, and make whole what has been smashed. But a storm is blowing from paradise; it has so buffered his naked behind that he can no longer turn. The storm irresistibly propels him into the future to which his back is turned, while the pile of debris before him grows skyward. This storm is what we call Bier Markt.

---

1 A situation that has changed somewhat in the intervening years. America is the world, and the last time I was in Paris I was served a concoction of Amaro Nardini, Fino sherry, Maraska, and Nikka From the Barrel (a high-proof Japanese blended whisky), which must be an indication of something.

2 Unfortunately, "classy" and "unfussy" can be hard to maintain simultaneously, as evinced by the bartenders' starched white chemist coats and the bar's "no shorts" policy grinding up against ten-dollar *chien chauds* and ubiquitous sports memorabilia.

3 Interesting fact that I learned from the Big Star documentary *Nothing Can Hurt Me*: in the early 1970s, TGI Fridays was one of the first bars in Memphis where one could order hard liquor by the glass, owing to a recently changed ordinance. Andy Hummel, Big Star's bassist, recalled, "Everybody who was the least bit interested in raising hell would be there."

4 Howard Pollack, *George Gershwin: His Life and Work* (University of California Press, 2007), 433.

Still, After All These Years

crapula (n) – "the sickness or indisposition following upon
a drunken or gluttonous debauch"

thus,

crapulent (adj) – "Of or pertaining to crapulence; suffering
from excessive eating, drinking, etc."...from Blount (1656):
"surfeiting or oppressed with surfeit"

There is also something quite satisfying about the employ-
ment of *indisposition* here. *Disposition*, of course, refers
to arrangement, order, being put-together, as well as to
temperament, but if one thinks also of *disposition* in terms
of what one is disposed toward, what one is prepared to
do, the use of *indisposition* to mean *unwell* becomes particularly evocative: to occupy a general state of not being
willing, prepared, or inclined toward anything. What better
description of the truly, wretchedly ill, or, more to the point,
the truly, wretchedly full?

I've been thinking of late about feast days, and my
misgivings therewith. I'll leave aside for the moment the
specific problem of Thanksgiving (cultural genocide, set-
tler colonialism, etc.) and keep things in the general terrain
of secular(ized) holidays that have the feast as a central
component. I have spent most of my adult life in Montreal
endeavouring to recuperate such holiday meals back into a
meaningful relationship with my and my friends' lives. You
know how it goes: "We, who are isolated by necessity, cir-
cumstance, or design from our families, and already skep-
tical of the trappings of this particular tradition, still have

an interest in forging new (or at least modified) traditions, returning to the ostensible spirit of the holiday (a celebration of each other, and of the food that sustains us), and of course taking advantage of a day off work, and so shall assemble anew and cram our gullets in common. To each, and each to their excesses, raise a glass." This is all well and good, to the extent that it comes off. However, just as often I have found the food becomes an impediment to the very connections I had so flattered myself as to declare the basis of my interest in the whole exercise.

Concerning spending time with those one cares about, any sort of meaningful engagement on an emotional or intellectual level tends to be eclipsed by the necessities of frantic food preparation, consumption, and recovery. I am not typically one to speak ill of overconsumption, nor of the demarcation of days devoted to its celebration, but it nevertheless has crossed my mind at more than one holiday dinner that those assembled in the midst of so many elbows around the table are so busy eating that little time is afforded to savour either the meal or the company. I suspect that a combination of the ritualistic gluttony of the holiday and a certain banality of its average fare produces this situation, in which we feel compelled to dispatch helping after helping of turkey (surely the most ponderous of possible birds) and mashed potatoes as if each time we are expecting to find writ across the freshly scraped surface of the plate some longed-for truth. It is the dissonance of a meal that is supposed to be "special," but is comprised of food that is so fundamentally boring that we feel compelled to plow through it, questing an ever-elusive satiety that we are denied and given surfeit in its stead. It is perhaps a mercy that we are too stultified by the end of the affair to acutely register our disappointment, instead mustering at best a pained sympathy for the others similarly indisposed.

The above might come across as somewhat snobbish. "Buddy's got a problem with mashed potatoes?" I hear you exclaim. But no, with the exception of turkey, I in fact like all of the "traditional" dishes of the ambiguously Anglo-Saxon Protestant milieu so familiar to white, middle-class Canadian thirty somethings: mashed potatoes are great (or can be, so long as the potatoes are subordinated to the true star, butter), I love boiled turnips and bacon, Brussels sprouts in almost any form, dressings and stuffings of various descriptions, but whether it is the vengeful spirit of religious observance scorned or just my own refusal to be happy, the meal so often feels like crapulence without succulence. Jonathan Meades has written similarly about Christmas,[1] and although his take is more polemic against the overdressing of the traditional British meal, his description of such holiday cooking as "centrifugal" strikes a chord for me (resonant, if not entirely pleasant). I have come to think of the holiday meal in terms of an "absent centre" around which the maelstrom of food and festivity swirls, a much-anticipated yet dismal scene from which one limps home and flops defeated into bed, uncomfortably full and yet curiously empty. But where is this absent centre? The turkey is there, the people are there. The snow is gently falling or finally melting or still well in the offing as the leaves clatter in the blazing multicolour trees. Perhaps what is missing is me. Perhaps I am merely horrible.

---

1 "Christmas Dinner with an Excess of Trimmings," *Guardian*, December 24, 2010.

A World Upside Down

Although I possess nothing approaching a collector's mentality (a hoarder's, maybe), it is reliably a source of excitement for me when travelling abroad to explore the vernacular chocolate bar selection. A recently discovered favourite is the United Kingdom's Toffee Crisp (no relation to the Coffee Crisp, one of my favourite Canadian chocolate bars). The bar is interesting not so much for its taste as for its structure, consisting of a lower layer of rice crisps held tightly in a sort of chocolate matrix, with a thickish layer of caramel (or, I suppose, toffee? What's the difference?[1]) on top, all enrobed in chocolate. I say it is "interesting" because of how the lower stratum breaks apart, crumbles in a way that suggests defeated masonry more than food, before one's top teeth have made it through the upper caramel level. I had no notion of how singular and almost disorienting this experience could be until it occurred. It is totally not what one anticipates, and very much gives one the sensation not of biting down but of *biting up*. The caramel is very chewy, and one is left with this resistant mass, the fragments of the crispy lower stratum scattered throughout it and about the recesses of one's mouth. Cool.

I have never had masonry crumble in my mouth, of course. Likely the closest I have come is the off-putting yet nostalgic grit of eating potato chips or a peanut-butter sandwich at the beach, but I like that kind of non-food evocation. For the sake of mixing Latin and Greek, let's call it a *paravictual* association: *victual* from the Latin *victus* for food, and *para* (to the side of, in proximity to but different from, sometimes against) because it concerns not only "non-food," but non-food that hovers around the periphery, enriching or defining the food experience. This is something I have thought about plenty as regards taste and scent—as with Scotches or wines that call up associations with things that one couldn't or wouldn't normally eat, like slate, or peat, or tar, urine, et cetera—but of course texture has much to contribute as well. Whether this is substantively different from referring to chocolate as "silky" or "velvety" is open for debate, but I think there is something more exciting going on when we are struck by manifest and perhaps incongruous non-food associations when eating, as opposed to calling on readily available analogies.

Viewed in cross-section, it is surprising how little of the whole is taken up by the Toffee Crisp's caramel layer, considering how thoroughly it dominates the eating experience. But, the allure of the cross-section as revelatory perspective aside (which is considerable, as histories of scientific imaging and theories of divine geometry in architecture/art history indicate), the tension between what is seen, what is felt, and what is otherwise "known to be true" about the bar is considerable. It is not the first time I have been given cause to reflect on the biting down versus biting up question, and why we think in terms of "biting down," when what actually happens is our lower jaw swings up and pushes food against our top teeth (the other time also involved a chocolate bar, and gave me a much-appreciated excuse to draw a *Mortal Kombat II* analogy), although it is only with the Toffee Crisp that the veil was torn away, so to speak, and I was confronted by the actual *experience* of biting up. It makes me wonder to what extent the Toffee Crisp was designed to produce this sort of somatic disorientation (my guess is not at all). And how generalizable is my own experience? Is something of the uncanny common to those eating a Toffee Crisp for the first time? Or every time, even?

If so, it would be such a tasteful and awesome gimmick to engineer into a chocolate bar. To, by a simple structural trick, provoke a subtle dis- or re-orientation of one's sense of one's body parts' relation to each other (one's body's relationship to itself, truly). I don't know much about neuroscience, but I imagine this has something to do with proprioception, the sense and sensors that allow us to know the relative positions of part of our body. So I wonder: in the case of biting down, how much of our actual experience of biting down truly *feels like* biting down, and how much is it just a conventional label on a still-opaque set of spatio-physical sensations, a linguistic gloss?

I suppose for my own sake I could try biting into a bunch of things and thinking really hard about how it feels, paying attention to how my upper and lower rows of teeth move through whatever it is I'm eating, but I could only generalize so far. Initial tests suggest that it feels like both sets of teeth are biting through/moving toward each other at comparable rates, but I don't expect that decades of discursive conditioning of somatic experience can be undone simply by *thinking harder* about it.

Ultimately, I am not really that invested in finding an answer, so much as I am intrigued by the further questions it can provoke. It is this uncertainty that attracts me in the first place, this lingering opacity at the centre of embodiment. Do I actually know how it feels to do this (bite down into a chocolate bar), or has it been eclipsed/constituted by my means of describing it? Or, leaving aside the old nature/culture imbroglio, how much does my identity depend upon proprioception, to say nothing of the entire sensory array that provides the experience of embodiment? Philosophers from William James and the phenomenologists up through Deleuze have been struggling with this for ages, and in recent years many of their dopey speculations have found increasing purchase in neuro- and psychological research on embodied cognition.[2] It is already well established that severe insults to proprioception, such as amputation or stroke, can significantly affect selfhood, but developments in embodied cognition suggest this process may be less facile—and less "social"—than simply "learning how to live with a disability." So what if we think of more mundane proprioceptive interventions and mediations in terms other than those of loss? Can a chocolate bar be a key to the corporeal spatialization of non-self-identity?

---

1 The inclusion of milk or cream (caramel) versus sugar and butter only (toffee), and differences in cooking time/temperature, apparently. I don't know if *toffee* as a term is regulated the same way *chocolate* is, and there seems to be some confusion as to whether this distinction is New World–specific, but let's say for the sake of simplicity that the sugary stuff inside the Toffee Crisp is what an American would likely call a very thick, chewy caramel.

2 See something like Andy Hamilton, *The Self in Question: Memory, the Body and Self-Consciousness* (Palgrave-Macmillan, 2013), or Shaun Gallagher, *How the Body Shapes the Mind* (Oxford, 2005), for recent philosophy-cum-cognitive-science discussions.

Monstrous Sympathies

Some years ago, I found myself in a small town on the Pacific coast of Mexico, in the company of a friend recently returned to the pleasures of seafood. He was fixated on the idea of eating as many urchins, prolific in the surrounding waters, as possible, yet mystified as to why urchins did not seem to already be a prominent part of the local cuisine. For, generally, things edible get eaten, particularly in poor towns bordering the bounteous sea. And, for an area renowned for its pig-stomach soup, we couldn't assume the absence was a matter of squeamishness.

I had my own mystery to contend with, and curiously, it was that of sympathy. I had recently read an essay in the 2006 *Proceedings of the Oxford Symposium on Food and Cookery* entitled "More Than One Way to Crack an Urchin" that provided a brief culinary and historical-naturalist overview of the *Echinoidea*. Within a scant few paragraphs of the author's statement that "The sea urchin is heartless, brainless, and otherwise lacking in organs that might inspire our empathy," I found myself strangely emotionally interpellated by the descriptions of these quite otherworldly-seeming creatures. In fact, I was beginning to feel quite guilty about the thought of eating them, but for the life of me I had no idea why. Why this irruption of sympathy for something like an urchin, rather than for any of the much more morphologically familiar creatures I eat on a regular basis? Even the smug vegetarian slogan "I Don't Eat Anything with a Face" excludes the urchin from serious consideration. Small wonder, for although it has something like a mouth—designated in still more strange-making language as "Aristotle's Lantern"—the urchin more resembles an artifact of medieval materiel (such as a mace or caltrop) than anything else that would confront us with the ineffability of the "fellow living thing." As such, it takes the Levinasian heteronomy of the Other into pretty far-flung ethical terrain.

And yet! I am suspicious that it may just be the wonderful strangeness of the urchin that excites this sympathy, some true sense of wonder at the alienness of its engineering—Five-fold-symmetry! An endoskeleton of crystalline plates! Transformation of aqueous CO_2 into solid matter!—so that it seems a shame to destroy such a weird, tiny creature. If this is the case, then it is effectively exoticism doing the work, and that is poor stuff of which to make a moral engagement, although I am hardly the first to succumb to the aesthetic exciting the ethical. Additionally, with its intensely Lovecraftian manufacture, the urchin seems like a little emissary from an ancient age or arcane lineage, and one should well know not to meddle with peculiar and paradoxical-seeming artifacts, lest one open the Gate and invite some perception-bending Nameless Mist into one's brain. Interestingly, this sense of the arcane and primordial is not at all universal among those who encounter the urchin; take, for instance, amateur naturalist W. N. P. Barbellion's impressions on his dissection of the thing, from his 1919 *Journal of a Disappointed Man*:

> Very excited over my first view of Aristotle's Lantern. These complicated pieces of animal mechanism never smell of musty age—after aeons of evolution. When I open a sea urchin and see the Lantern, or dissect a lamprey and cast eyes on the branchial basket, such structures strike me as being as finished and exquisite as if they had just a moment before been tossed me fresh from the hands of the Creator. They are fresh, young, they smell *new*.

When my own time came, I too marvelled at the alien-seeming complexity of Aristotle's Lantern, although there was not the same "scent of newness" that so captivated Barbellion. No less exciting, though, it remained as I had anticipated, ancient and perplexing, but also with the feeling that in cracking through that shell, breaking the carapace, one entered a world somehow untouched by the orders and organization of the surface world. The Kraken stirs, somewhere in the deep.

Maybe it is less the exoticism alone that touches me than the manner in which the urchin is dispatched, occasioned by the tragic ingenuity of its design: for fresh eating, what one has to do, basically, is stab the thing through the mouth (shattering Aristotle's Lantern) and, this purchase gained, crack its shell apart. For the mouth is the only unprotected, relatively fleshy patch available amidst of a battery of prickly spikes. And so I brush aside the queerly grasping motile spines, the nascent ethical impingement, to fixate upon an anatomical oddity in isolation. From monstrous sympathies to monstrous indifference. An animal made by human hands into an artifact. There is something sad and sort of poignant in a creature so seemingly well-arrayed for its own defence, undone by the anatomical extravagance of having a mouth. Perhaps, absurdly, it is this that awakened my sympathy in the first place: a cold, bristly creature doomed by its mouth?

Take That, Instincts

"Miracles of civilization," I calls 'em. The first time I tasted a really dry sherry, I had accidentally invited a couple of folks I barely knew to a wine bar in the East Village—I had no idea the place was a wine bar, and in fact had at the time never been to a wine bar (I think I vaguely imagined a bunch of business types sitting on leather banquettes drinking out of comically oversized glassware and listening to Thievery Corporation remixes of Antônio Carlos Jobim and the Sex Pistols). I was going on a second-hand recommendation for oxtail arancini, and I hadn't thought to ask any further questions about the type of establishment it was. So I showed up in my homemade Bolt Thrower T-shirt, hungover and vigorously unkempt, and hoped for the best. As it turned out to no longer be the nineties, however, I cannot nurture the illusion that I am anything other than exactly the kind of unkempt, hungover food fop such establishments intend to attract, so really I had nothing to worry about but my own looming insolvency.

For happy hour the bar was offering complimentary glasses of dry sherry, so obviously I took them up on it. I am to this day glad I did, because it was just so profoundly strange. But strange in a way that has become a very useful reference point for me, an almost perverse-seeming strangeness that has helped me to orient other tastes, other experiences, in wine and beyond. Because in a pretty undeniable way it sort of just tasted *bad*. Bad and weird, and not really like something human beings are supposed to drink, and yet (or of course) I found it totally intriguing and irresistible. I recall describing it as tasting "like someone had found a way to make paint thinner start to putrefy, but at the same time also taste good?" I have since learned many ways to make sense of this experience: that sherry is wine and comes from Andalusia, and exists in many styles and gradations; that the wine is often left to age for several years under a layer of living yeast; and that a similar approach to wine-making curiously flourishes over three thousand kilometres away, at the foot of the Massif du Jura on the eastern edge of France. And I have since learned to order this experience in terms of taste, and from the original "expired paint thinner" derive all sorts of other notes like hazelnut and sea water and citrus zest. But there remains a bizarre feeling of appreciation for the tremendous, creaking, contradictory machinery of socialization, of empire, conquest, trade, and trend, that has brought me to this drink, and this drink to my lips. For I have no doubt that I do truly enjoy it, that I'm not just putting on airs for the cat (who's not even very smart) or the pile of unread *New York Review of Books* in the corner, and there is something impressive and satisfying about being bound up in this mess that makes the genuine enjoyment of something so clearly derived from decomposing fruit a possibility. "The fact that I am enjoying this," I say, "is a miracle of civilization." I actually said that. To myself. And maybe the cat. And now I am saying it to you.

Aren't We All Feeling A Little Abused by Turkey and Peas These Days?

I may as well say right out that I am not a huge fan of poutine, even if I now and for the better part of my adult life have considered Quebec my home. I respect and appreciate it as a culinary phenomenon, but perhaps as my once-ardent love for french fries has receded over the years, it happened that I never found a place for poutine in my life, or on my plate. Nonetheless, a permutation of the dish that I can really get behind is the poutine galvaude. The galvaude is effectively the hot turkey sandwich of poutines, adding peas and shredded turkey or chicken to the already daunting mix of fries, cheese curds, and brown sauce. It has always struck me as the least offensive of variations, so much less so than the poutine Italienne, for example, which somehow manages to be so grossly unlike chili fries as to boggle the mind and belly alike. Although I had long presumed the "galvaude" to refer to a historical personage, perhaps the inventor of the dish, or an obscure region of either France or Quebec, upon further investigation it turns out to be so much more interesting (if slightly detrimental to my argument that it is somehow less disgusting than regular poutine):

galvauder (v) "Compromettre par un mauvais usage, en prodiguant mal à propos"

The rough English translation is something like "to sully, tarnish, waste, or squander," but it's really about ruining something by doing wrong by it, and I (as always) appreciate the deftness of the dictionary definition: "to compromise by a wrong or inappropriate usage, to squander wantonly."[1] Further context could likely be provided for me by a local (or perhaps a Gaspésienne, since I have heard rumours it is of such origin), but as it stands, it seems like *galvaude* is just a funny reference to abusing a poutine by subjecting it to turkey (or chicken) and peas, which is ironic, as poutine already supposedly derives its name, colloquially, from being a fucked-up mess.[2]

Quite by chance, however, I recently stumbled upon this entry for poutine in *Larousse Gastronomique*:

> A dish from the south of France, consisting of a mixture of tiny young fish, particularly sardines and anchovies, which are fried like whitebait. The name comes from the dialect of Nice, from the word *poutina* (porridge). Poutine can also be made with poached fish sprinkled with lemon and oil, and can be used to garnish a soup or fill an omelette.

An earlier source indicates that *poutina* refers to the name in Niçoise dialect for immature sardines, i.e.: whitebait.[3] Not that the regional polysemy of words should be news to anyone, but that Québécois poutine could be said to be a poutinization (i.e., mess) of the earlier Niçoise version of the dish, and poutine galvaude a further poutinization—indeed, a *galvaudisation Gaspésienne*—of "traditional" poutine, is, in linguistic terms, pretty cute. In addition, the poutine Niçoise, particularly when cooked into beignets, sounds delicious, and I wish it was as easy to find in dumpy neighbourhood diners as is its Quebec counterpart. Although, I guess if the poutine Niçoise was prepared with only as much care as the average poutine, we're probably better off without.

1 Thanks to Craig Schweickert for assisting with this translation, as I was floundering a bit with the specific and somewhat unintuitive negative sense of *prodiguant* as wasteful.

2 Charles-Alexandre Théorêt, *Maudite poutine!: L'histoire approximative d'un plat populaire* (Editions Heliotrope, 1997).

3 Georges Castellana, *Dictionnaire français-nicois*, (Éditions ludographique françaises, 1947).

From the Cauldron of the Speckled Seas

There are three key moments in the history of my relationship to whisky. The first occurred probably sometime around the turn of the millennium, when I still lived in Prince Edward Island. A friend who lived in a beautiful and expansive house in the country, and also benefited from her mother's habit of leaving town for summers at a time, decided to throw a "Scotch party," which, it was decided, would also be an "old-timey" party. We all dressed up and there were cards and billiards, and, of course, Scotch. In a relatively fortunate twist of irony, this was the one party that was ultimately broken up by some nosey noser of a neighbour, and I can imagine their perplexity upon finding the house populated by dapper teens in ties and evening dress, listening to ragtime and playing baccarat, in lieu of the pantslessness and pool-ruining and weed and irresponsible meat-cleaver brandishing that might have greeted them at any number of other parties throughout the summer. After most of the revellers were cleared out by this well-meaning dipstick who thought it a good idea to make a bunch of teenagers drive home from their "liquor-themed" party, my best friend and I found ourselves alone in the basement, finishing up our game of pool. Neither of us drank at the time, in spite of being in the twilight of our adolescence and otherwise quite ill-behaved, so we were mainly in it for the tie-wearing. But out of curiosity my friend took a swig from an abandoned glass, and him gagging violently and removing himself to the sink to thoroughly wash out his mouth provided my first association with Scotch as a thing.

More meaningful—in terms of taste, at least, rather than affect and nostalgic reverie—was when many years later

I, for the first time, tasted a well-made, well-aged single malt. The name isn't important, for at the time its identity meant nothing to me (actually, it was a Lagavulin sixteen year). I knew it was "good," and that it was expensive, but I approached it as an unknown entity. Not completely unknown, because I knew of course that it was a whisky, but in the initial tasting it opened up for me a space of the unknown. Which is to say that it did not immediately taste like anything I knew, anything I had ever drank. For a moment, the idea of what whisky was or could be was banished, replaced by this space of possibility, of uncertainty, of suddenly not knowing what it was I was tasting, and having to devote considerably more attention to its ascertainment than I was accustomed. This is now an experience I know well, where food or drink suddenly exerts a monopoly on the imagination: confronted by a wealth of intense and unfamiliar (or strangely familiar) tastes, time slows down, the moment distends, and we must focus all of our attention on what is happening in our mouth. In that first drink there is a swell, a disorienting pulling of focus, and the world recedes into the background.

The experience is all the more challenging because of the borderline familiarity and peculiarity of the flavours one encounters. Indeed, as I have come to know Scotch better, what is fascinating is how much of the tasting lexicon evokes aromas and flavours of things that one might never actually have smelled or eaten, and in many cases cannot or should not be eaten: tar, peat, straw, trawling ropes, scorched wool, brackish water, plastic buckets, and so on. To be sure, many of these aromas would be familiar to those who have spent time in, say, rural Scotland, or many maritime locales, but such direct experience is hardly prerequisite, for it is to a great extent in the mobilization of the imaginary that these tastes become intelligible as such. The imaginary—the sea, the peat, the tar, the whatever—comes to stand in and do some of the important associative work of tasting. It can be quite remarkable, and I appreciate Scotch, and to a lesser extent the culture of Scotch, for encouraging these flights of associative fancy that are nonetheless still ostensibly rooted in what is happening in one's mouth.

Many years later I found myself on the island of Islay itself, traipsing about quite improbably with a very tiresome Spanish leftist (the type of old-school socialist who talks a lot and tips poorly) and a charming if possibly evil Norwegian editor of a very exclusive Scandinavian luxury lifestyle magazine that, as I understood it, is all but hand-delivered by Slavic thralls to manor houses with dirigibles moored overhead. I had been thinking much about terroir and whether one can meaningfully speak thusly about Scotch, or any hard liquor production, for that matter. Although any credible definition of terroir must incorporate an element of culture, tradition, and human agency alongside the natural contributions of soil composition, climate, and the raw materials themselves (grape, grain, milk, what have you), there are questions as to whether in the case of something like whisky such nuances as the kind of water and the provenance of the grain are not stripped away by the harsh rigours of the distillation process. Are we speaking of the same register of terroir if something is merely made in a place, but not of the place?

I am inclined to think that the persistence of the specificity of such material constituents in the formation of the identity of the final product is important if we are to speak of terroir (or for the product to speak of its terroir), although I find attempts to reduce terroir to a collection of objectively measurable variables somewhat naive, or perhaps merely confused (whether trying to validate or disprove its existence).[1] While many of the distilleries on Islay (a sparsely populated island in the Southern Hebrides that boasts a whopping twelve single-malt distilleries) make a point of pride that their whisky is made completely with water drawn off the lochs of the island proper, the malt itself is often composed at least in part of mainland barley. So how might one speak of terroir if the very thing being fermented is the fruit of another land? One of the more compelling arguments for a physical terroir component to Islay whisky I've encountered is that the peat burned to give Islay malts their distinctly medicinal, smoky character is a composite matter, formed of naturally compacted and partially decayed grasses, leaves, moss, earth, seashells, and so forth. Feathers and bugs and bird dung too, probably. Thus, peat from Islay would (plausibly) differ from that of the Highlands, Speyside, the Isle of Skye, providing a sort of snapshot of each region's local biodiversity. A snapshot that you then set on fire, of course.[2]

It occurs to me, however, that so deep is the structuring dichotomy of nature/culture that even as I believed myself ready to see terroir as one of those deconstructivist always-already-both-natural-and-cultural hoozlewazzles I am always on about, I was still drawing the same old dividing lines in an attempt to keep "nature" on one side and human intervention on the other. If, by contrast, we turn the telescope (microscope?) around and start from the other end, take as our starting point the reality of terroir, and then see of what it consists, we arrive at a very different understanding of the thing before us. For terroir is of necessity an indeterminate thing (if it is a "thing" at all), not only because places and traditions and the people that people them change over time, but because we are always in the process of learning, being told, and deciding about terroir, and that education is in its way part of the production of terroir. Terroir is thus not only a product in part of human work, but of human thought, something we apprehend into existence. I can understand that some Chardonnay grown in the Jura (the French wine region, not the Scottish island just north of Islay) has a mineral quality reminiscent of some Burgundian wines, perhaps because of a similar latitude, proximity, and shared veins of marl and calcareous soil, and that whether intentionally oxidative or not, a nutty quality persists, perhaps due to idiosyncrasies in local winemaking practices so ready to hand as to be invisible to the vintners even as they practise them. And when a winemaker tells me that this cuvée has a particular quincey acidity because that parcel of grapes, that bit of (physical) terroir, sits at just such an elevation, shaded from the summer sun by the treed hillside opposite just so, I am learning something about terroir, in a very particular way. I can pass on this information in the form of technical miscellany to another, I could even go and visit to confirm and say, "Yes it is just so," because I am seeing it and I have been told what it means.

Or I can sit in a pub in Port Ellen and watch the old men try to flick their beer tabs into a glass behind the bar, listening to a friendly, brassy local proclaim, with the latent Gaelic lilt that undergirds the frank, ready wit of the Ileach, her preference for the French over the British ("At least they're bloody Celts!"). Then I can walk out the door and smell the soft smoke of the malting plant, look at the ocean, and the line of distilleries hugging the shore, with their intentionally drafty barrel warehouses taking what they may from the wicked wind, the stinging brine. Then I can think about taste of place, and I don't think I've learned anything less about what terroir means.

1 Geneviève Teil has written on this issue in wine: "No Such Thing as Objectivity? Objectivities and the Regimes of Existence of Objects" in *Science, Technology & Human Values* 37(478), 2011.

2 Of course this would only hold for peated malts. Peat-smoking is most intensively practised in Islay, and while it is not unheard of elsewhere in Scotland, it accounts for only one aspect of a whisky's character.

The Sixth Quarter

As we have seen in recent decades, not only have the demand for wholesome foods and the obsession with health and environmentalism not meant a return to "traditional" products and processes (although the image of tradition is successfully marketed) but it has accelerated, and will continue to accelerate, the improvement, the enculturization of nature drawing on tradition as a resource to be selectively improved. [...] Traditional taste poses a challenge not a threat to technoscience; the more one specifies what is missing from the new product, the more the civilizing process proceeds. Tomatoes aren't what they used to be? But you don't like bugs either? Let's see what can be done. A company in Menlo Park is perfecting a bioengineered vanillin, one of the most complex of smells and tastes. Scientists are approaching museums armed with the PCR technique, which enables them to take a small piece of DNA and amplify it millions of times. This recovered DNA could then, at least in principle, be reintroduced into contemporary products. If eighteenth-century tomatoes are your fancy, there is no reason a priori why one day a boutique biotech company aiming at the Berkley or Cambridge market couldn't produce one that is consistently pesticide resistant, transportable, and delicious for you—and those just like you.

—Paul Rabinow[1]

To put this quote in context, one must understand that when writing of the "enculturalization of nature," Rabinow is not talking about nature as an ahistorical, universal given, but a nature that has come to be known, described, and effectively constituted by generations of theologians, romantics, naturalists, and scientists; a nature the knowing of which has a history. Nature, historical inquiry tells us, is a moving target. So when does a food cease to be natural? If we accept that a degree or quality of human intervention is likely to serve as the deciding factor, how much is too much? When did we break the chain, fray the thread that could have connected the tomato of today (or tomorrow) to its prelapsarian past? At the dawn of agriculture? Of horticulture? When exploration, trade, colonialism, and conquest spread beasts and seeds far beyond the terrains where they were formerly found? As the industrialization of food systems began to accelerate in the interwar years, with their attendant infrastructures, advances in transport and refrigeration that reshaped the kinds of foods we could grow and want and keep? Or with the advent of biotech, that penetration beyond the veil of the flesh, into the shadowy sub-cellular domain secret even to Nature herself?

I'm sure I don't know. And frankly, I'm not sure I care, although I am likely not alone in feeling somewhat uncomfortable about the prospect of this "boutique eighteenth-century tomato," not least because it seems the paramount expression of the sort of fey, fetishistic preoccupations of foodie culture. I am admittedly excited by the prospect of recapturing seemingly lost strains of various plants (and animals) to reinvest diversity and historical perspective into foodscapes that have over time been increasingly homogenized by the exigencies of grand-scale agriculture and distribution (even as such foodscapes have also been diversified by circuits of international trade). The fruit of a younger land and all that. Although, of course some similar such work can be achieved by just finding such heirloom plants and planting more of them, or prospectively by projects like the Svalbard Global Seed Vault in Norway. At the same time, this biotechnical optimism seems somewhat suspect and, like many very forward-looking accounts of the promises of genetic engineering, a touch reductionist. Could it take only a bit of Jurassic Park–style polymerase chain reactin' wizardry to conjure such snacks out of the hoary mists of time? Is the secret of that eighteenth-century tomato truly destined to be but a genomic divulgence?

My mind strays to David Cronenberg's horrifically gleeful exploration of mis-phylogenation, his 1986 remake of *The Fly*. Specifically the scene in which Dr. Brundle (Jeff Goldblum), attempting to perfect his teleportation technology, sends a steak through the device, for Ronnie (Geena Davis) to compare to another, un-teleported, steak:

Brundle: Now, I want you to try this, the teleported half.
Ronnie: Are you serious? A monkey just came apart in there.
Brundle: Baboon. Eat.
Ronnie: (takes bite of steak) Oh... Ooh, tastes funny. (spits out the steak)
Brundle: Funny? How?
Ronnie: It tastes um...synthetic.
Brundle: Mm-hmm.
Ronnie: So, what have we proved?
Brundle: The computer is giving us its interpretation of a steak. It's, uh, translating it for us. It's rethinking it, rather than "reproducing" it, and something is

getting lost in the translation.

Ronnie: Me. I'm lost.

Brundle: The flesh. It should make the computer, uh, crazy. Like those old ladies pinching babies. But it doesn't, not yet, because I haven't taught the computer to be made crazy by the flesh. The poetry of the steak. So, I'm gonna start teaching it now.

The steak in this case is not a copy—or isn't it? A translation, a transportation? Is it like a twist on the old Ship of Theseus problem, where this time one deconstructs the boat in one fell swoop and then rebuilds it with all the *same* parts (also known as the "Harry's New York Bar, Paris" problem)? Or, like in the early years of the Internet, when it was considered entertainment to enter a phrase into Babelfish, then copy and paste its translation and translate it back, to marvel over the fundamental non-equivalencies of the given languages and the incapacity of the program to grasp the nuances of syntax, let alone idiom? If what is missing, all other information intact, is the poetry of the steak, the poetry of the tomato, of what does this poetry consist?

Consider another case of what could be thought of as the enculturization of nature: vat meat. Or whatever you want to call it—in vitro or cultured meat seems accurate, and prevalent in the literature—I am not sure why "vat meat" has always stuck in my head. In any case, I am talking about meat grown in a laboratory setting, independent of any living whole of an animal. In recent years, there has been much buzz about in vitro meat: environmentalists and animal rights advocates have long argued that a cultured meat alternative could alleviate the mounting environmental costs and sheer moral burden of meat production. In

2008, PETA announced it would offer a $1 million prize to the first lab to develop commercially viable in vitro chicken; in 2013, Dr. Mark Post of Maastricht University in the Netherlands unveiled to much ado his fully lab-cultured hamburger patty; and culinary biotech start-ups such as Memphis Meats and Modern Meadow have plans to offer in vitro meat products as soon as, you know, it becomes financially viable and/or remotely delicious.[2]

These are the basic (practical) issues with cultured meat—cost and taste. For all that culinary pundits bemoan the blandness of the North American palate, meat itself remains a fairly complex product. The technology for producing in vitro meats borrows a basic technique ubiquitous in the scientific study of viruses and bacteria, and indeed all sorts of pathology: the cell culture. Cells are harvested from a host animal (typically stem cells, favoured for their growth productivity, although some researchers are attempting to move toward muscle cells as the *materia prima*) and placed in a nutrient-rich medium in which they are encouraged to reproduce. The process is complicated, but currently involves growing these cells into long, extremely thin strands that can be woven together to form something approximating meat.[3] However, meat is not just a mass of undifferentiated living tissue. As the variation in the taste and texture of different cuts of meat demonstrates, factors such as exercise, how the muscle is used, fat content (an engineering challenge unto itself), and what kinds of minerals and nutrients are provided by the circulatory system all play a role in defining the characteristics of a piece of meat. Suggested workarounds for this hurdle include electrical stimulation, or the use of a sort of scaffolding to "work out" the meat matter:

In order to produce three-dimensional in-vitro meat, it is necessary to have a scaffold. The ideal is an edible scaffold that would not need to be extracted from the end product. To simulate the stretching that muscle cells undergo as a living creature moves around it is highly desirable to develop a scaffold that could periodically shift its form thus "exercising" the cells. This could be achieved by using a stimuli-sensitive scaffold made of alginate, chitosan or collagen, from non-animal sources. The scaffold would then stretch periodically in response to small changes in temperature or pH levels.[4]

In the absence of an edible scaffolding, we are left with the idea of some sort of apparatus, mechanical or electrical, by which these sheets of tissue might be exercised into something resembling meat. A vital prosthetic of sorts, in an inversion of the usual sense of the word—a prosthetic body for phantom flesh, as opposed to a prosthetic limb for a living body. There is considerable overlap and sharing of ideas/expertise between the fields of in vitro meat and regenerative medicine; researchers at the Wake Forest Institute have already developed an Integrated Tissue and Organ Printing System to 3-D print simple physiological structures out of bone, cartilage, and muscle tissue.[5] Rather than producing an artificial limb, they, along with the culture and the laboratory itself, could provide the artificial conditions of vitality by which this organic material can hope to organize itself into meat.

Somewhere around the point of writing the phrase "a prosthetic body for phantom flesh," I begin to wonder whether my assertion that "the natural is a moving target" is irrelevantly academic. But if the notion of a wad of tissue grown in a nutrient medium in a warm, meticulously sterile laboratory setting is unsettling, we might pause to ask ourselves what is more fundamentally "natural" a process than cells dividing and taking what they need from their environment? Just as the cell culture relies on its nutrient medium and its stimulus scaffold and the entire apparatus of the lab for its survival, so too does the animal of our organic idyll rely on its ecosystem, the plants and earth and air that surround and sustain it; just as the more typical meat animal relies on its factory farm, its feed, and its hormone and antibiotic shots, its materiallyconstrained mobility, and eventually upon the complex of skills and machineries that render it ultimately as meat.

Nevertheless, I am susceptible to the suspicion, bordering on a conviction, that however skilfully engineered, however many hurdles overcome, the in vitro meat, like Brundle's teleported steak (and perhaps Rabinow's boutique eighteenth-century tomato?), will taste somehow funny, somehow *wrong*. Uncertain about my priorities, I slide from the ethical allure of meat without killing to the aesthetic (or existential? I can't always tell the two apart) discomfort with flesh never subjected to embodiment. So is this a perverse lack of empathy? A fetishistic insistence on the priority of organismic unity? The vat meat lacks even the embarrassment of offal; it is a part from no whole. The sixth quarter. Once alive, but not a life. What is wrong with this meat? "It's got no brain, no blood, no anima!" exclaims the increasingly frustrated fictional everyman before me. I realize that it may merely be a matter of romanticism, a newfangled yet old-fashioned notion that the poetry of the steak lies not in some anima or soul, but very imprecisely in its material entanglements, in all their messy contingency and unpredictability. Can the lab be made crazy by the flesh?

In 1931, Winston Churchill, writing for the popular science-fiction newspaper the *Strand*, imagined that fifty years hence:

> We shall escape the absurdity of growing a whole chicken in order to eat the breast or wing, by growing these parts separately under a suitable medium. Synthetic food will, of course, also be used in the future. Nor need the pleasures of the table be banished. That gloomy Utopia of tabloid meals need never be invaded. The new foods will be practically indistinguishable from the natural products from the outset, and any changes will be so gradual as to escape observation.[6]

I don't know why Churchill didn't think to write "dystopia" in lieu of "gloomy Utopia," but I can tell you that what I am really holding my breath for is less the triumph of cruelty-free meat than the advent of the boutique restaurant, which, for a modestly exorbitant fee, will take a sample of your DNA, splice it into the in vitro meat's germ-line DNA, then exercise and age the shit out of it, so that six months later you can walk in and have a burger that, in so eating, takes a bite out of you.

---

1 "Artificiality and Enlightenment: From Sociobiology to Biosociality," *Essays in the Anthropology of Reason* (Princeton, 1996).

2 "Lab Meat: Tastes Like a Million Bucks," PETA, April 21, 2008. The award has since been withdrawn. See also: Peter Singer, "The World's First Cruelty-Free Hamburger," *Guardian*, August 5, 2013; and Alok Jha, "Synthetic Meat: How the World's Costliest Burger Made it onto the Plate, *Guardian*, August 5, 2013.

3 Michael Specter, "Test-Tube Burgers," *New Yorker*, May 23, 2011; Maddie Stone, "The Future Will Be Full of Lab Grown Meat," *Gizmodo*, May 27, 2016; *Future Food*, "Cultured Meat; Manufacturing of Meat Products through 'Tissue-Engineering' Technology."

4 http://www.futurefood.org/in-vitro-meat/index_en.php

5 William Herkewitz, "Incredible 3D Printer Can Make Bone, Cartilage, and Muscle," *Popular Mechanics*, February 15, 2016.

6 "Fifty Years Hence," *Strand*, December 1931.

Merry Effing Christmas, or, Giving Rum Another Chance, or, Rum Gives Me Another Chance

Here is a simple winter cocktail: take equal parts Campari, Italian vermouth, and dark rum, with a few dashes of a reputable chocolate or *mole* bitters, if you have one on hand. Stir with ice, strain, garnish with orange. It is a good cocktail. It has depth and character without feeling overactive in the mouth. I am, as an oft-bent rule, not a great fan of rum, but here it plays well with the other ingredients, and the voices of the various spirits are harmonious. I have heard it called a number of names, I appreciate "Man About Town" for its evocation of the Boulevardier—one of my favourite cocktails—with which it has much in common, but it was first introduced to me as the Negroni Hivernal, and for me it will remain so named.[1]

The name feels both appropriate and counterintuitive. Gin, which would usually anchor a Negroni, has, in spite of its summer-drinking and British colonial associations, a wintry quality. Cold, clear, coniferous—at least, I often think gin and think winter, and vice versa. I also think gin and think of drinking it on the rocks at a long-ago staff Christmas party in a four-storey lesbian bar, because I had worn out my nerves on just about every other spirit available, and for the first time it occurred to me that gin might be a nice thing. Rum, on the other hand, is a hot Caribbean spirit that nevertheless thrives in the winter by virtue of its brown sugar/molasses/spice profile. If only because I don't much like drinking rum in the summer, it feels right to make of this darker, deeper, spicier riff on the Negroni a cold-weather friend.

Jonah Campbell

The cocktail also makes me think of how I used to like rum. More specifically, it reminds me of what and of whom I most often think when I think of rum and liking it, and also of Christmastime and liking that (for underneath it all I am a grossly, if intermittently, romantic fellow). Once upon a long time ago, I decided that it was worth attempting to befriend this person with whom I'd previously had some passing but pleasant interactions. We knew one another from parties and through mutual friends, and she had eyes that were kind of sleepy like a cat's eyes, but precisely in the way that a cat's eyes can be at once sleepy and burningly, terrifically alive. Intelligent, perceptive, tricky eyes. I called her up one day and she said yes, she would love to hang out, but unfortunately was moving to another country the following week, but I should come to her going-away party (she lived, it turned out, on the very same street as myself, but below the tracks, whereas I lived above). I did, and it was enjoyable, and I probably talked a lot about *Frankenstein* or maybe not much at all, and when next we spoke she said, hey, how about this, how about next time we see each other we just pretend we are already good friends, and then let the getting to know one another happen from there? What dispirited lump of a human could resist such a proposition? Not I, thankfully.

When she returned to the city for a visit many months later, around Christmastime, she invited me for a late-night walk "with a bottle of brown in the neighbourhood she once slept in and now misses in slight brown ways" (the invitation was couched in the third person for, I assume, poetic effect). I was appropriately stoked. The bell rang sometime late, and when I opened the door, before I could even greet her, she slipped on the ice and fell down the stairs, of which, thankfully, there were only three, but I assure you it made an impression. I'm not very good at telling stories, I realize, but this is important. She had with her a bottle of rum, and we sat on the floor in my dim, Christmas-lit living room, drinking brown liquor, eating snacks (I don't remember what), talking about theory and listening to Björk[2] until we were very rum-warmed and somewhat drunk. Then we took an old saw and went into the touchingly, embarrassingly picturesque, lazily falling snow to steal a branch out of which I could make myself a modest Christmas tree, in that neighbourhood where I too no longer sleep and also occasionally miss in what maybe I can call slight brown ways.

---

1 First served to me by Matthew Perrin, of Lawrence Restaurant in Montreal. Thanks, Matt.

2 The album *Telegram*, which always reminds me of Christmas. I must have been fifteen, in Prince Edward Island, at the big old house my parents have since sold and about which I am sometimes nostalgic. My older brother was home for the holidays, and someone (probably my mother?) was like, "Hey, why don't you guys dress the Christmas tree? At least *pretend* to have some holiday spirit?" So we did, and listened to the just-released *Telegram* while doing so, and it was nice.

Aim Low, That the Chariot May Swing to Meet Your Mark

"It tastes like licorice," the girl said and put the glass down.

"That's the way with everything."

"Yes," said the girl. "Everything tastes of licorice. Especially all the things you've waited so long for, like absinthe."

"...I wanted to try this new drink. That's all we do, isn't it—look at things and try new drinks?"

—Ernest Hemingway,
"Hills Like White Elephants" (1927)

The above might well be the bleakest, most succinct expression of existential malaise of the whole damned Lost Generation, but it still hits close to home, perhaps a little too near the contemporary bone. I personally derive a significant amount of pleasure and affirmation (existential, even) from the trying of new drinks, at least some of the time. Which may not say much for my spiritual health (I mean, I also like books and smiling dogs squinting in the sun), but it suggests at least that I suffer little *mauvaise foi* in my dilettance.[1] At some point, in the midst of the semi-intentional self-sabotage of my academic career and listless pursuit of literary recognition, it occurred to me that *dilettante* may well best describe my situation in, and relationship to, the world: a confusion of soft skills and partial knowledges, unified only by their status as interests I have failed to pursue to the point of expertise (and the possibly mistaken impression that they add to my charm). This could have been a disappointing revelation, given that *dilettante* probably hasn't been used as a positive descriptor in the past 270 years, but, like *amateur*, *dilettante* proves to have a kernel of etymological honesty in it. Roughly the same kernel, in fact. For where (as is fairly obvious) the root of *amateur* is *love*, and its essence to do something for the sake thereof (contrasted with the expert or professional), the root of *dilettante* is *delectare*—to delight. Historically, the dilettante delighted in art, specifically, and like the amateur was so driven not by professional (read: "serious") aims or expectations, but by the sheer joy of the thing. If *delight* seems like a fluffy word, that is perhaps a good thing. The inability to pin down the qualities that make something delightful may be part of the charm. And while *love* and *pleasure* are not far removed, both have the tendency to grow stiff and calcareous with the serious discourse that accretes around them. Which is not to speak unilaterally ill of seriousness; indeed, there is certainly something to be said for the gratifications of pleasures harder-won, but the love of pleasure and the love of love can be quite ponderous things in the absence of delight.

In the early eighteenth century, the Society of Dilettanti was formed in London by a group of dukes and scholars and other professionally moneyed layabouts (NB: moneyed layabouts by profession, as opposed to professional Classicists) to appreciate and promote the appreciation of Greek and Roman art, but equally to do so in a spirit of light heartedness and considerable inebriation. Horace Walpole described them, I suppose disparagingly, as "a club for which the nominal qualification is having been in Italy, and the real one, being drunk," although this reeks somewhat of the triumphalist moderationism that mistakes the result for the object and reduces everything else to mere pretext. The dilettante understands, contra Brillat-Savarin,[2] that just because one has ended up sotted, distended, and groaning with one's take, it does not mean one failed to truly appreciate what was put before one. But the world despises a dabbler, and the dilettante remains hated for loving, unwanted for wanting.

Actually, that may not be true. For what has the age of the Internet, lifestyle entrepreneurship, and gutted pensions brought us but the exaltation of the non-professional expert and the professional dabbler? An author-turned-publisher-turned-cabinetmaker-turned-contractor friend pointed out to me that there's probably not a barber, bartender, or small business owner under the age of thirty-seven in any urban centre who doesn't have a creative writing degree and a stack of unsold hardcore records clogging up their crawl space. A valid argument that demands a modification of my own. Which modification might consist in forcing a distinction between the dilettante and the amateur: I think that passion—driving passion in particular—is importantly absent from the portrait of the dilettante: if we are surrounded by affirming messages exhorting us to "Find the one thing you love more than anything else and do it for the rest of your life" (barf), we less often hear the call to "Find a thing that is interesting and pursue it until your interest is exhausted, I guess" (if there were a little more mingling of these messages, we might have a very different romantic culture, to boot). I am arguing here for the legitimacy of being compelled in a pursuit not by passion per se, or professional dedication, but by appreciation; to be comfortable with something less than mastery of an art or the all-consuming fire of devotion. To quote the etcher, failed poet, part-time essayist, and art historian Philip Gilbert Hamerton, "If the essence of dilettantism is to be contented with imperfect attainment, I fear that all educated people must be considered dilettantes."[3] To make peace with imperfection may be as much a mark of maturity and calmness of spirit as is great diligence and rigour. All of which to say, I think I might try making my own vermouth. Praise be to the bright generalist!

---

1 I cannot get out of my head the suspicion that Sartre's *mauvaise foi* (bad faith) was a pun on *mauvais foie* (bad liver), given that both the French and the English share a historical belief in the liver as the source of courage (see lily-livered or *avoir les foies blanc*), and *mauvaise foi*, by way of some oversimplification, amounts basically to a form of intellectual/existential cowardice. Also, I like to make drinking-related jokes about *mauvaise foi*, as one might expect.

2 "Gourmandism is an impassioned, considered, and habitual preference for whatever pleases the taste. It is the enemy of overindulgence; any man who eats too much or grows drunk risks being expelled from its army of disciples." "Meditation 11: On Gourmandism," *The Physiology of Taste* (1825, translated by M. F. K. Fisher, 1949).

3 *The Intellectual Life* (Macmillan and Co., 1873).

Fine-Tuning the Contours of Realness

i. The Abyss of BBQ

In the world of chips, there is a phenomenon known (exclusively to myself, until now) as the "Abyss of BBQ." The phrase "Black Hole of BBQ" might do just as well, but I have always been a fan of abysses (invoking them, staring into/being stared back at by them, tossing my hopes, dreams, and expectations into them, etc.). The Abyss of BBQ describes the tendency of many exploratory and unconventional potato-chip flavours to end up tasting like a variation of a generic BBQ chip or, at best/worst, like BBQ bordering on All-Dressed. Which, I suppose, given that All-Dressed by definition contains BBQ, would just be "Half-Dressed." In recent years, the second (or third) wave of the novelty-chip renaissance has started to, as it were, "chip away" at the phenomenon, but the Abyss nevertheless exercises its attraction.

Travelling outside of North America exposes one not only to a plethora of new chip flavours, but to a different set of culinary reference points around which the local canon of flavours constellate. The most jarring of which, particularly where the Abyss of BBQ is concerned, is the fact that BBQ is not a tried-and-true point of reference for potato-chip flavour design (or consumer familiarity) the other side of the Atlantic. This is a reminder of how distinctly American is BBQ/barbecue (or, to be really accurate, African, then African American, then Ugly American), both the chips and the culinary technique/culture to which they so tenuously and non-specifically refer.

Arguably, BBQ flavour in North America refers to nothing (for the sake of clarity, I'll take "BBQ" to indicate

Jonah Campbell

the chip flavour, and "barbecue" the culinary practice, although we'll see how long it takes for that neat distinction to collapse). It points to no specific meat, to no specific seasoning, thus belying the considerable diversity that exists in American barbecue (to say nothing of commercially available barbecue sauces that present a simulacral register unto themselves). It points only to the chip itself, or the idea thereof, such that any chip flavour that invokes a particular barbecued food item, such as ribs or, say, baby back ribs (the imaginative capacity of chip-flavour scientist-administrators for what items can be barbecued is strikingly lean, it seems), is inevitably understood as a variation on the pre-existing ur-flavour of non-specific BBQ. Which, perhaps to its credit, is not even itself a single uniform flavour, since every brand's take on BBQ falls somewhere or other along a spectrum of sweetness versus smokiness (ultimately tasting like Mrs. Dash, with more or less smoked paprika involved). It is thus extra-specially conceptually interesting to encounter BBQ chips in Europe or the UK, because one can't help but wonder whether their reference point is the American BBQ chip or some notion of American barbecue as a culinary entity proper. Put another way: is the European BBQ chip a barbecued-meat-flavoured chip or a (American) BBQ-chip-flavoured chip? It is not always clear.

To take the case of the British version of Smoky BBQ Kettle Chips, one gets the sense that there is perhaps a "real thing" that the Kettle UK creative team is attempting to approximate, but it is as if they assume that the American BBQ chip is itself an approximation of some truly existing object called BBQ (rather than the self-contained simulacrum I am suggesting they represent) and they in turn are trying to get closer to that Real. In effect, the UK chip tastes like a more carefully refined version of a BBQ chip. But what could I possibly even mean by that? It's just less gross, less vulgar, than the typical American BBQ chip? It tastes like more real things (like, plants and shit) went into making this chip that is supposed to taste like what? A condiment? A process? Like fat and fire and the transformation of time into the relaxation of flesh?

My friend James has suggested that the appearance of the BBQ chip in the UK is an indication of the extent to which the usual British resistance to American cultural influence is being dissolved by the recent trend in burger and "American barbecue" joints popping up around London (see also: the proliferation of beers that don't taste like malty dishwater, for better or worse). I am inclined, though, to speculate that the American BBQ boom is more the result of forward-thinking entrepreneurs realizing the opportunity presented by all these Britishers eating BBQ chips and being like, "By Jove, these are good, but...barbecued what?" And so I am left wondering, to what does the UK Kettle BBQ chip refer? Some local interpretation of the "American Grill" or to yet some other chip referring to a chip, in a chain of imitation extending toward an ever-receding horizon, over which peeks a suburban dad in a suspiciously pristine apron that reads "In Dog Beers, I've Only Had One"?

ii. On the Science-Fiction Turn in Chips

Perhaps I give potato-chip scientists too much credit. I think I have a tendency to imagine them as a league of poor man's Ferran Adrià, dog-eared copies of Philip K. Dick novels in the pockets of their lab coats, eager to probe the limits of representation, memory, and experience at the intersection of sensation and technology. For chips have become a bit of a technology of the fantastic. For all that cultured meat and genetic engineering have a *holy shit it's the fuckin' future* quality about them, potato chips evoke more of the actual imaginary of science-fiction past, by which I mean space-food pills, those condensed meal-in-a-pills perhaps best remembered from *The Jetsons*, but with a lineage extending as far back as the late nineteenth century. One could argue that diet shakes and nutritional supplements are likelier candidates for the realization of this vision, but I think that the space-food pill is about more than sustenance and nutrition abstracted from the material particularities of food, because one is always given to believe the pill reproduces something of the specificity of the food it is supposed to represent. The space-food pill may also be thought of as a fantasy of harnessing the imaginary of food, or at least one that poses the question "Is there something that eludes us still in the experience and the enjoyment of food, even when we have produced a technology that not only mimics the taste, but generates the impression of having eaten the thing?" David Cronenberg would answer yes: it is the "Poetry of the Steak," or, that which allows us to be *made crazy by the flesh*.[1]

Of course, chips fall well short of this. They are a comparatively primitive technology, hewing all to one side of the sensory/sustenance divide, and even then to flavour over feel. Over the past decade, however, we have witnessed something that could be called by way of shorthand "the science-fiction turn in chips." For a long time, North American chips were dominated by condiment flavours, many that already had a place relative to potatoes in their various preparations (e.g., ketchup, salt and vinegar, sour cream and onion). There are, of course, exceptions, and many would remember the brief explosions of precocious creativity that brought us pizza, hot dog, roast turkey and stuffing, and, uh, boloney chips, but for the most part the roster remained somewhat stable, if not conservative (excepting the notorious Hostess fruit flavours debacle of the late 1970s). In recent years, however, the market has been deluged with new flavours, such that it seems an impracticable as well as worthless undertaking to stay abreast of them, let alone offer any critical commentary. What is noteworthy about this phenomenon is that on the whole there has been a move toward the representation of more complex foods, entire meals even, and this, I argue, brings the chip more in line with the spirit of the space-food pill. Although not actually a potato chip, the Doritos Late Night All-Nighter Cheeseburger flavour was the first chip that for me imparted a sense of the uncanny, and while this effect has been by no means uniformly achieved in the waves of subsequent experiments, the anticipation of its possibility has at least been routinized. The idea that a chip could be eerily reminiscent of the thing that it supposes to imitate, even when that thing is a salad or a sandwich of some complexity, has been elevated from the utterly implausible to the merely improbable in a strikingly short time.

I like to think of those flavour scientists toiling away, impelled at least as much by their desire to advance the practice of their art as by the caprices of cool-hunting marketing executives. Perhaps a rung or two lower on the visionary ladder than the Wendell Stanleys and Frank Macfarlane Burnets who pursued the question of whether or not viruses were alive to the logical extent of destabilizing our very understanding of "life" itself, but scientific adventurers nevertheless. If they are mere technicians, then they are technicians of human experience.

And so, when I encountered the new Old Dutch Bacon Cheeseburger Slider chips, my initial reaction was to be infuriated—was Old Dutch seriously presuming to claim that their chip tasted not simply like a bacon cheeseburger, but like a *miniature* bacon cheeseburger? What hubris, I fairly spat. Such airs! Upon further reflection, however, I came to appreciate the possibility that this was more than base pandering to the popularity (already waning, I should think) of the slider, that there was something of an intentional provocation about it. I found myself charmed by the idea that such a fine distinction was not in fact meaningless, for it prompts one to say, "Okay, of course not. But what if?" What if there was a way to capture the nuances of space and scale on the plane of a chip? What if more than taste could be conveyed in a flavour? What if you could make something taste *small*?

Unfortunately, the chips in reality are basically horrible. Over seasoned, under theorized, vulgar and shitty, as with the rest of the Double Dutch "Appetizers" line (Burstin' Onion, Buffalo Wings and Blue Cheese, Calamari and Tzatziki). What inspired puckishness I inferred is likely totally misplaced, although I do appreciate the ambitiousness of deciding that "fermented milk, garlic, and mollusks" or "county fair whole deep-fried onion" were flavours within the scope of the practically attainable. Ironically, the line's greatest failure is not in the domain of taste, but in everything else about the chips: thick-cut, wide-wale rippled chips, the seasoning powder caked on, cloyingly dense, somehow achieving simultaneously the impression of dehydration and dampness. It makes a wretched offering. I've always been a fan of plain, myself.

---

1 See "The Sixth Quarter."

My Body, Which Is Given For You

There is something in the tearing of fresh pita bread that feels like the desire for flesh. It is like a soft leather. The dry dusting of flour on the surface may not, unfortunately, yield to my organicizing notions, but pita nonetheless persists for me as the most *animal* of breads. It contains hints of some imaginary or platonic form of skin, an analogy or synecdoche for life. It is the skin of some mythical pre-Christian beast. One side peels, delicately, from its opposite, as skin peels obligingly from muscle. But they are all the same surface.

I am not the type to hone in on the erotic qualities of food, for all my gastronomic preoccupations, but there are other pleasures of the flesh that reside in Eros's shadow, lost in the eclipses of sex. I am suddenly struck by the ambiguity of the phrase "pleasures of the flesh," for it denotes both the pleasures arising from the flesh of the subject and those deriving from the flesh of the object, and the pleasures themselves oscillate wildly between the two. The erotic does not exhaust the carnality of food, just as it does not exhaust the pleasures of the flesh. Because for all that it immediately invokes sexuality, *carnal* has meant *meat* as long as it has meant *sex*. Flesh and blood, making people crazy. Brundle knew it. Perhaps most satisfying: in this separation we find the desire to bite through something finally liberated from the necessary constraints of sex.

On Food, Film, and the Documentary Mode, in Two Takes

i. Kings of Pastry, 2009. Directed by D.A. Pennebaker and Chris Hegedus

So *Kings of Pastry*, more or less as promised, provides an engaging, entertaining look at the Concours Un des Meilleurs Ouvriers de France (MOF), which is less a competition in the "there can be only one" sense than it is a sort of final exam in excellence for pastry chefs, a more exclusive and prestigious red seal for the profession. The characters are likeable, the human drama compelling, the tension high, and yes, as promised by the promotional copy, there are lots of grown men crying. Altogether, though, what *Kings of Pastry* fails to be (in my opinion) is *interesting*. To be fair, I don't think this was the directors' goal in the first place. It fits comfortably into a particular mould, a popular subgenre of the modern food documentary, the hero's quest. The narrative of obsession, the precarious balancing of family life and emotional health with devotion to one's craft, are all familiar and effective. But the film is not really *about* obsession, it doesn't think about obsession—it merely features it. Neither are we are given any particular insight—or maybe only the barest flashes—into the world of pastry and *pâtissiers*, and for a film about people striving to be the "best craftsmen in France," we learn very little about the craft itself.

Perhaps my critique stems from the fact that a significant portion of the documentary is devoted to sugarcraft—the elaborate, delicate showpieces of the competition, the sugar-and-chocolate sculptures they call *bijoux*—rather than to pastry proper. These are the great crowd-pleasers, of course, truly astonishing feats of ribbon and blown-sugar confectionery, but of somewhat less interest to me because they are effectively inedible (also stupid-looking). Some time is devoted to the cakes, tartlets, and various *choux* that populate the other categories of the MOF, but for the most part these magically appear on the screen; we do not see how these creations, the products of great artistry, training, and practice in their own right, come into being. They are the quotidian fare of *pâtisserie*, fading into obscurity beside the glitz of the showpieces that in their unchecked alienness and tasteless (post)modernism begin to remind one of a Delia Deetz sculpture.[1] The bulk of the craftsmanship highlighted in the film concerns itself with turning food into nonfood (well, to the extent that pure sugar is "food"), and in the end, the craft of pastry is rendered no less opaque than at the outset.

One of the most interesting moments of the film, which passes almost unremarked, occurs in the opening scene, as part of then-President Nicolas Sarkozy's speech at the MOF awards ceremony: "There are not two forms of intelligence, two kinds of skill," Sarkozy states. "Manual skill does not fall from the sky any more than an intellectual skill. I don't want any more of this concept in our country. Because this idea is morally scandalous." In the new France, the France of today, the hard work, devotion, and skill of the craftsman/worker (*ouvrier*) shall be respected, the artificial separation of these labours collapsed. But where and how shall this be recognized? Certainly, the MOF must master every element of the craft, but there is a certain irony that this valorization is conferred in a context where the craft is shown at its most rarefied, that only where the presentation is so abstracted from eating and food becomes (visual) art, that the craft is said to reach its apogee.

I do not intend this as a polemic against the *pièce montée*, and I have no firm opinions about the relationship or distinction between craft and art. Without the decorative flourish, I would have a pretty insubstantial skeleton of a life. Carême's famous dictum that "The Fine Arts are five in number: Painting, Music, Poetry, Sculpture, and Architecture—whereof the principle branch is confectionary" underlies *Kings of Pastry*, but I have to wonder what, in this formulation, is architecture assumed to be for? To house? Or to materialize some sacred geometry or social order? And subsequently, what is pastry for? What is it supposed to *do*? Merely to dazzle? If so, fine. A similar question could be asked of the documentary, and if the answer is merely to entertain, also fine.

At one point, the head judge of the MOF states, "each product is a moral dilemma." That he's talking about a cream puff makes this cute, a perfect hyperbolic statement about the high stakes of the MOF. But what are the stakes, exactly? The men competing have devoted years of their lives in preparation, and to wear the stripes of a *maître ouvrier* has considerable career implications, but that is not all he is talking about. The politics of French food are fraught and complex, and very overtly tied to French national identity. It is no accident that the collar that only *les maîtres ouvriers* are permitted to wear bears the French tricolour. Is the moral dilemma one of the dignity of the profession at war with human sympathy, the need to judge impartially in order to protect the standards of excellence (and by extension the dignity of the nation)? Is it thus, writ small, about patriotic duty struggling with one's basic fraternal co-feeling?

Pennebaker and Hegedus, who also made *The War Room* (1993) about Bill Clinton's 1992 presidential campaign (as well as the 1967 Bob Dylan doc *Don't Look Back* and a slew of other music documentaries), choose not to consider these questions. They seem interested in neither the stuff of the trade nor the stuff for which it might conceivably stand, but in something that I suppose is called "human drama." Perhaps I should not begrudge *Kings of Pastry* for not doing something it was not intending to do. In the spirit of the good documentarian, the duo profess that their approach is strictly "observational," but the Michael Moores of the world aside, this is what so many documentaries presume to do already. Indeed, it is the premise upon which the genre is founded: to present things as they "really happened." The observational mode, however, does not erase authorial agency, even if it seeks to obscure it. Someone still decides where to point the camera, decides what stays in and what gets edited out. There is no view from nowhere.

Certainly, some of the competitors featured in *Kings of Pastry* are genuinely sympathetic, but I nevertheless left the theatre feeling that the whole thing was a trifle (pun intended) superficial. It remains a sort of anonymous human drama wherein one encounters the characters very much as dramatic placeholders who move only for the mechanistic unfolding of the plot. Even the subject itself feels like a placeholder. It could feature any men (men specifically: as of 2010, there were no *meilleures ouvriéres* in pastry), in any grueling trial, risking any everything. There is triumph and tragedy, but little exploration of pastry as a craft, an esoteric set of manoeuvres and the traditions, institutions, appetites, and desires that give them meaning. But I don't suppose my complaint that I was hoping for a more incisive analysis of the cream puff will be widely shared. Out of good taste and respect for, I don't know, I guess emotions as a thing, I will resist the urge to pursue further the analogy between human drama and blown-sugar treats that are seductive but ultimately undigestible. But you know I'm thinking it.

ii. El Bulli: Cooking in Progress, 2010. Directed by Gereon Wetzel

In quite another vein is Gereon Wetzel's *El Bulli: Cooking in Progress*. Many of the reviews I encountered before watching the film suggested it was a little on the boring side, but I think that this may be why I enjoyed it as much as I did. In fact, it may also be why I might consider it such a "good" documentary, as opposed to "such a documentary," as I feel about Pennebaker and Hegedus's *Kings of Pastry*. It is exactly this foregrounding of human drama and its articulation within a narrative arc that is absent from *El Bulli: Cooking in Progress*. The film is not an exposé, nor an exhaustive how-it's-made procedural breakdown, but it is nonetheless very much about the work of El Bulli. El Bulli *in process*, not solely *in progress*, as the title declares.

The double meaning of "cooking in progress" is apropos—chef Ferran Adrià (who helmed the restaurant from 1997 until its closure in 2011, and with whose name it has become synonymous) conceived of El Bulli as an avant-garde restaurant, and was explicitly concerned with advancing the field. Under Adrià's leadership, El Bulli enjoyed the reputation for many years as the best restaurant in the world, and remains a landmark institution for the approach to cooking variously dubbed "molecular gastronomy" and, more recently, "culinary modernism."[2] "Have we done this before?" is the question that echoes throughout the film, throughout a creative process that is at the same time concerned with not succumbing to the allure of the merely novel. Whether Adrià succeeds in avoiding the trap of cooking that is clever yet devoid of substance is not for me judge, as I never have and never will eat at El Bulli, but Wetzel—director of *How to Make a Book with Steidl* (2010), a film about the art of making books about art—manages to capture and communicate this tension in subtle but effective ways. The film is almost a technical drama, lingering over the careful deliberations of Adrià's creative team, their experiments, discussions, and negotiations, with each other and with the ingredients that they are transforming. There are no talking heads in *Cooking in Progress*, no confessions, no expository dialogue to break up the (slow, deliberate) "action," as it plays out over the course of three acts.

The film opens as El Bulli closes for the season, with the team packing up their equipment and moving to their lab in Barcelona. This is neither metaphor nor affectation: the research space of Adrià's inner circle—Oriol Castro, Eduard Xatruch, and Eugeni de Diego—is both laboratory and kitchen, with burners and skillets, thermal immersion circulators, and nitrogen baths in equal measure. Here they will spend the next few months working with various ingredients to see what can be done with them. No menus are assembled; there is only a highly methodical free play with the properties of various foodstuffs. Free in the sense that the conventional limits of the food (both in terms of culinary use/application, and of actual physical properties) are disregarded, or at least re-evaluated, although the strict assessment, detail, and inscription of the results of the experiments places a different set of constraints upon the activity. It is a sort of operationalized, material brainstorming.

Following this, we return to Catalonia, to Cala Montjoi, the site of El Bulli, where preparations begin for reopening the restaurant: the training and organization of the staff, the assembly and fine-tuning of the menu, the arranging of stones. Finally, we see the restaurant in progress, although only in a very restricted fashion. Rarely are we shown the patrons in the act of enjoying their food; they arrive, take pictures, revel in the aura of the establishment, and while they eat, we retreat to the kitchen, where dishes are constructed, expedited, and perpetually re-evaluated. It is during this sequence that we have the least sense of time. Are these the services of a single night? A week? A month? Several months? Suddenly, it is October, the season winds up, the staff begin to close the restaurant down, and the film ends on exactly the note upon which it opened. We realize that what we have been watching is an exploration of the routine—it is not a tale of genius or mad science, the spectacular fancies of high gastronomy, but of the routine work that goes on behind the glittering, variegated, often quite challenging facade.

If there is a climax to the film, it can be identified only retrospectively. In a late scene, at the end of a seating, Adrià calls to Castro something to the effect of "Hey, Oriol, this year we can still keep up." The film ends five minutes later, in a quiet montage of delicately staged menu photography, and one realizes that this was the resolution of whatever dramatic arc the film has accommodated, as well as a summation of Adrià's own personal mission as a chef with El Bulli, and the aporia at its heart. Keep up with what? Indeed, the majority of the emotional tenor of the film is provided through the handful of subtle exchanges amongst Adrià and his team. Scenes where one tastes some preparation, a dish or component thereof, and in the moments of silence that follow, the audience feels the egos at work, the economy of creative energy, the authority and ambition, all through a protracted stare or averted gaze. The result is not

Jonah Campbell

melodramatic (there are no chilling canned strings or a *Law
& Order*–esque knell to signal the import of the situation)
so much as it is even slightly absurd in its portentousness,
and this awkward comedy ultimately lends the movie a lot
of its charm.

For all the behind-the-scenes action, however, the actual
functioning of El Bulli remains somewhat abstruse. We
see some of what goes into the dishes of vanishing ravioli,
parmesan crystals, and minted ice lakes or whatever, but
a mysterious quality is retained. Wetzel himself has said
that "it is the lacuna that I like, the vacuum of representation."[3] It gives the interested party just enough to see how
the spirit is enmeshed with the instrumentation, without
becoming lost in technical detail. Thusly is the mystique
of the restaurant allowed to persist. "There's no trick," the
film seems to say, "it's just a simple trick!"

I expect that this measured, unsensational approach to
the documentary may not be for everyone, but I found
it quite refreshing. One doesn't leave the theatre feeling
like one has been told a tired story by way of a cinematic
machinery at pains to proclaim its unvarnished verité. In
a strange way, Wetzel manages to give life (a human life)
to a subject matter that, like Adrià's denatured creations,
could seem quite cold and unapproachable, both alienated
and alienating, and does so without resorting to the broad,
garish strokes of documentary bathos. I suppose I can't say
much more than that *El Bulli: Cooking in Progress* is interesting if you are interested in that sort of thing. Although I
didn't think I was, really, until it turned out that I am. Ha.

1 *Beetlejuice*, dude.

2 Molecular gastronomy, as an abbreviation of "molecular and physical gastronomy," was coined by French physical chemist Hervé This and the Hungarian-born Oxford physicist Nicholas Kurti in 1988, and elaborated over a series of publications. "Modernist Cuisine" is a more recent appellation advanced by Maxime Bilet and tech entrepreneur/ patent troll Nathan Myhrvold in their 2,438-page, 52-pound tome of the same name.

3 Interview with Gereon Wetzel by Ohad Landesman, www.ReverseShot. org, July 27, 2011.

On Something Wholly Other Than the Documentary Mode: Louis XVI Eats a Tomato

Jean Renoir has been called a lot of things: secular saint, father of the French New Wave, the greatest of European directors, et cetera. In 2008, Peter Bogdanovich, in an article for the *Observer*, called him "The best director, ever." As much has been made of Renoir's transcendence as of his humanism, but part of what makes his work so captivating for me is that his humanism is precisely *not* a grand, universalizing, triumphant humanism, but is of a rather inauspicious and quotidian variety. To this extent, I feel more comfortable proclaiming that it is less that his films are *humanist* than that his characters are profoundly *human*. Disarmingly, vitally human. I do not mean that they are "flawed" (the usual unimaginative shorthand implied by "human") but that they are believable in a way that reminds one that the usual believability of cinematic characters is itself an achievement wrought through our collusion with cinematic conventions and the suspension of disbelief (a collusion I find increasingly dishonourable as screenwriting becomes increasingly shitty). They do and say things that we do not as film viewers expect them to do or say, but that make them seem more human, less clever fictional constructs. This in turn produces the suspicion that they may actually live on in their worlds without us, rather than live only in and only for the film and its duration. This, at times, produces an erratic quality to Renoir's films that is familiar because it evokes something of the churning irrelevancies of a real, live human life, while remaining entirely within the strictures of narrative filmmaking.

There is a striking scene in *La Marseillaise*, Renoir's 1938 film about the French Revolution (coyly subtitled *A Chronicle of Certain Events Relative to the Fall of the Monarchy*) where, well into the insurrection and with the storming of the palace close in the offing, Marie Antoinette enters a room to find the king eating a dish of tomatoes:

> Marie Antoinette: My lord, you're eating in spite of the circumstances?
> Louis XVI: Why shouldn't I? The stomach is an organ which ignores political nuances. I asked for tomatoes. People have been talking a lot about this vegetable since the people from Marseille have arrived in Paris. I wanted to try it. Well, Madame, do you want to know what I think of it? It is an excellent dish, and we were wrong to disregard it.

No additional context is provided for the meaning of this exchange, save that in an earlier scene we hear the men from Marseille (volunteers in the revolutionary army) asking for tomatoes at a restaurant. Modern audiences might not realize that tomatoes at the time were hardly considered a food across much of France (as well as England, Canada, and the United States), in spite of their being consumed widely in the Midi, as well as in Spain and parts of Italy. Popular opinion, or at least popular aristocratic and botanical opinion, long had it that tomatoes were probably poisonous, and at the very least disgusting. Their association with the hot-blooded republican peasantry sporting their red Phrygian caps made the tomato a fine revolutionary icon, an association strengthened by the influx of tomato-eating Southern maniacs into Paris in July of 1792.

And so, in this scene we are given to enjoy what passes as both a genuinely human moment and what might seem testimony to the utter cluelessness of the king in his royal isolation. Or, taken another way, as a signal of the king's growing cognizance of the political forces that are set to overtake him. Certainly, the ability to take a moment amidst the tumult to enjoy a nice mesal is symbolic of the corruption and complacency of the monarchy, indeed the entire ruling class. But the look of what might be defiance, admonishment, even suspicion, that he darts at his wife as he utters this last "Ils sont un met excellent, nous avons eu tort de les négliger" is perfect, and intimates that he is speaking of something greater than an error of taste. He's talking about taste, he's talking about tomatoes, he's talking about the revolution, he's talking about hunger, but we are not beaten over the head with it.

La Marseilleise is a pretty triumphant film; it's about *liberté*, *fraternité*, and *égalité* more than it's about Robespierre and the Terror, but I want to resist saying it's a political film in the usual sense. Okay, it is definitely a political film, definitely an ideological film, in the way it chooses to bring to us the emancipatory message of the French Revolution through the activities and accidents of the average dopes on the street, rather than focusing only on the big historical figures. But it is not one that attempts too neat or seamless a hegemonic effect. It is nuanced, and there is a friendly irony; the story, underneath all the songs and slogans, is, like the people who populate it, too complicated. In "Renoir and Plotless Cinema," Jonas Mekas writes:

> Renoir's people look like people, act like people, and are confused like people, vague and unclear. They are moved not by the plot, not by theatrical dramatic

climaxes, but by something that one could even call the stream of life itself, by their own irrationality, their sporadic, unpredictable behavior.[1]

"The awful thing about the world," observes Renoir, speaking through the character Octave, whom he himself plays in *La Règle du jeu*, "is that everyone has their reasons." This is not the Reason of the Renaissance, brimming with liberatory promise. The genius of Renoir's humanism is not the exaltation of these or any particular reasons, but that he makes a virtue of acknowledging them. That virtue, I suppose, is sympathy.

---

1 *The Village Voice*, July 1961.

His Measure of Her Powers

Not long before his unfortunate, untimely death, *Esquire*'s food editor-at-large Josh Ozersky published an essay, "Consider the Food Writer," that declaimed what he saw as the continuing influence of M. F. K. Fisher on food writing in America. In it he declared that if the genre was to emerge from a creatively stunted and parochial bourgeois hegemony, "M. F. K. Fisher must die." Figuratively, of course. Fisher has been literally dead since 1992.

On the one hand, I agree. Or, to put it more carefully, I share Ozersky's distaste for the prevailing narrative and stylistic conventions of much contemporary food writing. His critique is pretty on point:

> They all grope for depth, via tropes that are now pretty much obligatory. The author will find in some plate of pie a memory of mother and, later, in the act of their own eating, a universal experience that binds us all together. Somewhere in there will always be found some fond memory of a picturesque past or exotic land, some unforgotten tomato or miraculous couscous that still reverberates, even today, and underscores the persistence of the past and the brotherhood of man.[1]

In this way, the unwavering predictability of the form threatens to eclipse—or effectively render irrelevant—the actual content. Like the ready-made drama of a bad food documentary, the specificity of the life, the food itself, the creepy ephemerality of experience, all are made pat. Undeniably, after the first or second go-around, this becomes boring, and usually trite, and undeniably this is *part* of

M. F. K. Fisher's legacy. Hers was a voice that defined modern American food writing, and Ozersky is correct that she occupies a privileged position as the godmother of the genre, universally lauded by foodies and food writers alike. I can hardly take issue with the critical reconsideration of one of the giants of one's genre. I also think that Ozersky's compact analysis of the emergence of a particular, class-bound relationship to food (food eating, food thinking, food writing) in the 1960s and '70s, as a precursor to the modern "food culture" phenomenon, is valuable, especially as it emphasizes the publishing infrastructure behind these developments.

On the other hand, I think Ozersky is a bit of a fucking fouler, who should maybe fuck off and, you know, check himself (not to speak too ill of the departed). Let us leave aside for the moment his summary dismissal of Susan Sontag as irrelevant and banal whilst lamenting that Fisher may not be so casually dispatched, if only to say that while I am not always a fan of Sontag, to glibly dismiss her work on the representational violence of photography, or illness as metaphor, as merely part of an "indistinct din" of mid-century writing interesting only to cultural historians seems almost comically boorish. His estimation of M. F. K. Fisher's own literary powers is somewhat confused, and this produces ambiguity in how he characterizes the consequences of her influence.

Ozersky opens with the pro forma admission that Fisher's merits as a writer are besides the point, which implies that it is her legacy with which he is solely concerned, although this is not exactly so, given that he spends the rest of the article waffling between begrudgingly acknowledging her talents and declaring her work saccharine, superficial, and dull. He grants that she is at best an able epigrammatist, but, personal differences in my and Ozersky's literary tastes aside, I think he gets her all wrong. I have always found that it is precisely in isolated quotation that Fisher's true strengths as a writer are least discernible, and run most toward the "superficially profound," as Ozersky claims. It should not be necessary here to mount a lengthy defence of Fisher's writing, but I think where she succeeds most is as a literary stylist who is able in still relatively short passages to communicate a frank and disarming—and, perhaps most importantly, unpretentious—sensuality. As one who considers himself an unfortunate, impoverished anti-sensualist, locked in a garbled and loathsome relationship of mutual misrecognition with his own body, I am not easy to impress on this front, and I am almost embarrassed by my appreciation for Fisher's work in this respect. If the aphorism is a form of compressed wit, I would argue that it is in her longer passages that the aesthetic richness of her prose is given space to unfold. Even if at times her romance is too high for me, I recognize something special there, that is more than the "treacle" of Ozersky's evaluation. But anyway, to each their own. I get it.

What leaves me feeling most uneasy about Ozersky's piece is that underpinning his call for what is in effect a dirtier, more conflicted, grotesque, and perhaps pedestrian—if not populist—food writing is a very peculiar construction of what contemporary mainstream food writing looks like. His dystopian hegemonic landscape is populated by the likes of Ruth Reichl, Elizabeth Gilbert, Kim Sunée, Amanda Hesser, Julie Powell; the heir(esses) of Elizabeth David, Judith Jones, Julia Child. If this list seems gendered, it is not even so conspicuous for who is included, but who is absent. What about Anthony Bourdain, who is inarguably as great an influence on the voice of twenty-first-century food writing as Fisher? What of Calvin Trillin, Adam Gopnik? Michael Pollan and Mark Kurlansky? What of Harold McGee, or professional bad boys Marco Pierre White and David Chang?

Why do these names—some chefs (professional or celebrity), some historians, some critics, none (save McGee, perhaps) innocent of participating in the tired narrative bathos of memorializing their first oyster/summer strawberry/fermented chick embryo—not appear in Ozersky's portrait of the food-writing oligarchy? Certainly, one can't exclude any of these bestselling and James Beard Award–winning authors from the culinary cultural mainstream. And yet they are identified neither as part of the problem of rule nor even as aspects of a solution, however problematic. Indeed, in spite of their success, these big names remain strangely invisible in Ozersky's account:

> I've read moving and resonant accounts of eating, scenes that rang true from my own experience and that of other dirtbags like me. But I've never read them in a glossy food magazine, nor can I think of a single one that ever got nominated for an award... There remains an immense, seething, varied, noisy, conflicted, confused, unclassifiable population of people who eat, and cook, and for whom food isn't a source of community—at least not with that elite class of mandarins that currently control the field. They can all be heard, but they can't get published or paid, which makes them invisible and unviable, voices in a wilderness that need to be heard. There is no doubt in my mind that if Fisher were alive, she would champion them. But she isn't, and her legacy suffocates us, immobilizes us, covers us as tightly as the tenderloin in a beef Wellington. Food writing today is one great echo chamber, and the voice it echoes must be silenced.

This passage speaks to me. I am as tired as anybody (as or more tired than Ozersky, even) of the unexplicated, unproblematized mobilization of "community" and the trope of food as a mutually intelligible universal in food writing; food is paradoxically the great leveller and the great divider, debaser, destroyer. Food is a shibboleth. Food is a problem. And it is not for this that people call themselves "foodies." But with the scene as he has set it here, Ozersky's argument for inclusion seems more akin to a backlash against the ascendance of what is pejoratively called "Women's Fiction" in food writing. Indeed, it reads less like a plea for the inclusion of more diverse voices and experiences than a demand for the suppression and erasure of what Ozersky identifies outright as an educated, independent woman's perspective. The interrogation of the formulaic and trite is perhaps everywhere some kind of literary obligation, but to cast this mode as a gendered hegemony held in place by a bourgeois female editorial class—as similarly powerful "serious" male writers recede from the analytic frame—is just gross, and we can do better.

---

1 "Consider the Food Writer," *Medium*, October 7, 2014.

The Whole Beast Beyond Even Its Borders

I have been reading Fergus Henderson's *Nose to Tail Eating: A Kind of British Cooking*, and I am enjoying it to an uncommon, unforeseen degree. I am not typically a great appreciator of cookbooks. I picked up *Nose to Tail* because I recognized it as a classic that I had never investigated, and it seemed an essential volume for thinking through the contemporary resurgence of "craft" butchery. Indeed, it may be the very wellspring of that phenomenon where Anglo-Occidental culinary culture is concerned, Henderson and his London restaurant St. John being one of the first bastions of the trend of offal appreciation and "whole-beast" cookery.

What is truly impressive about the book—as much as, and perhaps in spite of, its tremendous impact—is the tone and spirit with which the whole thing is imbued by Henderson. *Nose to Tail* is disarmingly frank and warm, the prose elegant but utterly unpretentious. This is perhaps a too-worn trope in the description of good cookbook authorship, but it does more than anything feel as if one is being addressed by a friendly acquaintance of whom one has asked simple instructions for the preparation of an unfamiliar cut. The recipes are clear, not too clinical, and have about them a tremendously inviting quality, evincing a respect for both the reader/cook and their ingredients. The introduction by Anthony Bourdain aside, the book is free of the sort of orgiastic, high-sensualist, macho hyperbole that proliferates in much of the discourse on whole-beast eating. Henderson's is not a gastronomy of unbridled carnivory or an exultation of the excesses of the flesh—the dishes, while certainly meat-centric, are not excessive, but are presented as a part of the everyday, if an everyday that has come to seem sadly distant and inaccessible for many. One wants to try the recipes, not because they present a challenge to be met and mastered or an ethical promise to be fulfilled (there is none of the pedantic moralizing of someone like Hugh Fearnley-Whittingstall, although I do believe there is a place for that), but because reading them one is given to think, "Why wouldn't I try this?" Dishes are described as "sustaining," "steadying," or "a very good dish if you are feeling a little dented." Henderson tends toward understatement, in several instances describing recipes as inspired by previous meals to which he admits they likely bear no longer any authentic relation (but are delicious nonetheless), and in one case proclaiming a dish to be "based on a very dour recipe" (for Pea and Pig's Ear Soup).

Henderson also expresses his admiration for curly parsley, for its strong flavour and structural abilities, which I find particularly gratifying given that my own preference for curly over the widely endorsed flat-leaf variety has long made me feel something of a pariah and/or bumpkin. Further points in his favour are awarded for his use of the terms "lights" for lungs and "pluck" for organs all still attached in an organized fashion, terms I had no idea were still in modern usage; and for his enthusiastic recommendation of Fernet-Branca as a cure for any overindulgence (albeit with the caution "Do not let the cure become the cause").[1]

When years ago I dined at St. John, on my first visit to London, I was familiar with none of this, and I don't think I quite got it. I knew nothing of the restaurant or of Henderson save their importance to the "scene," with which I was by that time semi-acquainted, and I could appreciate that importance in a vague, historical way. But on the whole, I found the meal a little dull, especially in comparison to some of my other outings that same trip. I remember we had bone marrow, and perhaps a very large crab, and something involving a lot of braised kid. I don't know if I would come to an altogether different conclusion now, but I am certain it would be a different experience. I would like to chance it. To see whether the simplicity and forthrightness of the cooking might have a different effect on me if I were thus prepared for it. It brings to mind re-watching a film that perhaps one knows relatively well but has not seen since one has come to know and care more about form and context, or about film qua Film and a given movie's place therein. Not long ago I watched *Citizen Kane* for the first time in probably ten years, and was basically shitting my pants from the very opening: The camera rolling through a miniature Xanadu, conveying the same subtle horror by way of meticulous, abandoned opulence as the unchecked natural overgrowth of Manderley in the opening pages of Daphne du Maurier's *Rebecca* (although this effect is less pronounced in Hitchcock's adaptation). The rather mundane point being that having a better sense of the animating philosophy of a thing, its history, and the conditions of its production can often lend another quality of enjoyment to one's experience of (although conversely, "unmediated" experience has its merits, too, of course, of course).

Least anticipated, and perhaps provocative only because upon encountering it I am so surprised not to have encountered it so articulated before, is Henderson's statement of philosophy of nose-to-tail cooking and the place of vegetables therein. Mindful of the carnivorous overtones of his approach, he takes pains to declare: "There is equal respect for the carrot; once radishes are eaten, their leaves are turned into a peppery salad...they all *make up the whole beast*" (emphasis mine). This somewhat counterintuitive assertion that vegetables et cetera are part of the whole beast is more than just an injunction to Eat Your Vegetables and not throw shit out that could be good for something; it pays a deft homage to the very contingency of life. And, if one chooses to so take it, it serves as a reminder that whole beasts are never wholly or solely the beasts they are taken to be, but are deeply implicated in and made up quite literally of other life-worlds; they are not only meat, but guts and blood, plants and bacteria, punch-outs of ecosystems. They are stuff, yes, but stuff and relationships. Matter that may not be so easily disentangled, or may only be disentangled at great cost, from the worlds of which it is a part. If one is alive to it, the threads of relationality, and even a casual assumption of material agency (although this is not so foreign to culinary discourse), can be discerned running all through his book: "Do not be afraid of cooking, as your ingredients will know." Preparations must often be given just enough time so that ingredients get to know one another, time for the (savoury) pie filling to find itself. The "whole beast" thus materially and conceptually extends beyond the borders of the organism itself, comes to know itself in its relation to others, and of course vegetables form a part of that. But you know, all this coming from a guy who includes a recipe for Warm Pig's Head under "Salads."

---

1 I long thought the unlikely hangover remedy of Fernet-Branca and crème de menthe over ice, a favourite of most of the chefs I know, was a Fergus Henderson creation, or at least one of similar recentness. Imagine my surprise when I stumbled upon this passage in the 1954 edition of Elizabeth David's *Italian Food*: "For mornings after I have Italian friends who swear by a grisly mixture of Fernet Branca and Crème de Menthe; the appearance of the drink is that of a stagnant pond, and its effect depends upon individual reactions to shock treatment."

Tomorrow Might Not Come, If I Don't Let It

I ate pizza-flavoured Doritos once, sitting on the warm roof of a half-mangled pickup, in a parking lot somewhere in Maine. It was late and warm, and we were singing songs to stay awake, and jogging around the truck at every rest stop, feeding on the stimulation of the variety of fluorescent lights. It was a hot May, I don't remember what year, but I remember the Doritos tasted of pizza pockets.

So ready and specific an association at hand, I wonder whether this did not occur to the makers. But then, who "makes" a Dorito? Where in the network, the chain of translations, is the decision made what a chip "is," or what it is supposed to be? Was there a moment when, during the fine-tuning of the nth iteration of summer 2013's limited-edition Pizza Dorito, an adjudication was made as to whether the flavour was more pizza or pizza pocket, along with a calculation of the relative market potentials of each? One would almost expect the latter to win out, so receptive of novel, snack-themed snacks are contemporary audiences perceived to be. Maybe it didn't come to mind. Maybe, in their heart of hearts, they wanted to produce an evocation of a good pizza, of a better pizza than a pizza pocket, or a mini-pizza (worse still), an icon undiluted by microwave convenience. I was reading Proust's *In the Shadow of Young Girls in Flower* at the time, and thinking about David Lynch, for the first time ever. Lynch, in *Lynch on Lynch*, describes the genesis of the infamous Red Room of *Twin Peaks*:

> One night at about 6:37 p.m. in the evening I remember it was very warm. Duwayne Dunham and his assistant Brian Burdan and I were leaving for the day. We

were out in the parking lot and I was leaning against a car—the front of me was leaning against this very warm car. My hands were on the roof and the metal was very hot. The Red Room scene leapt into my mind... For the rest of the night I thought only about The Red Room.

Hands on a (warm) hard body. Proust rendering momentary impressions in elaborately exploded view, so thoroughly as to reveal what is in fact not there. Pizza pockets. Mosquitos. You, drunk, smashing bugs with your face on a screen door.

To Your (Spiritual) Health

If you are a regular reader of the *Guardian* (which I am not), or spend much time reading about the politics of clinical trials (which I do), you have probably heard of Ben Goldacre. Goldacre is a British physician and science writer who holds a post at the Centre for Evidence-Based Medicine at Oxford, and who for almost a decade wrote a *St* column called Bad Science, which he has spun out into several books. He writes well, has a quick wit, and while I sometimes find the rhetoric of his crusade against "bad science" sort of frustrating and tiresome, I can't help but feel a sense of kinship with someone I see as a fellow complicater (a 2014 collection of his writing is titled *I Think You'll Find It's a Bit More Complicated Than That*). He can, at times, come across as a typically smug scientific triumphalist, as in his crusades against pseudoscience and various alternative therapies (I personally have a bit more time than he for alternate modes of knowledge-making), but he is nevertheless no stranger to the complexities of evidence production. He is also a driving force behind the AllTrials and OpenTrials campaigns, which together have been advocating—with surprising, if achingly slow, piecemeal, success—for a research culture/infrastructure that would ensure that all clinical trials are centrally registered and fully report their methods and results, and for such material to be available to all researchers in a collaborative, open database.[1] You may be surprised to hear that no one is keeping track of the research conducted on drugs and other medical treatments that may or may not be approved for human use. The fact is, there are several such registries, but in spite of registration being mandatory in many countries, it seems people don't really use them.[2]

Jonah Campbell

Anyway, Goldacre comes to mind because it appears that the sort of do-gooding, new-leaf-turning, care-of-the-self jibber jabber that typically reaches fever pitch around January 3 every year has become a steady, unceasing drone in my social circles of late (perhaps it is called being in one's middle thirties?). As someone who has perpetually (or at least regularly) miserable health and for whom nothing in particular in the way of diet, exercise, vitamins, regular blood work, or homeopathic hoozlewazzle has ever made any difference, and who has by profession become rather intimate with the maelstrom of contingencies, fine-tunings, and epistemically rationalized fudgings that undergird the production of all scientific knowledge (not just the pseudo-scientific kind), I find the Ouroboros of everything-bad-is-good-for-you/everything-good-is-bad-for-you that fuels the endless peripeteia of health advice pretty obnoxious. And so it was nice to stumble across a *British Medical Journal* article of Goldacre's from around Christmastime a few years back wherein he takes lightly to task the kind of research (and subsequent marketing) that supposes to justify such things as chocolate and red wine consumption:

Moderate red wine drinkers, we are specifically informed, come out better on all kinds of health measures, and nobody wants to ruin Christmas by mentioning confounding variables again (like how moderate red wine drinkers hang out at home with their friends eating salad and talking about their posh jobs and stable social support). A fairytale science story must be simple, reductionist, and mechanistic. Red wine is good for you because it contains life-giving molecules, like antioxidants. And nobody wants to spoil Christmas—for the whole family—by mentioning that the antioxidants story is one of the great unspoken non-starters of twentieth century medical research... Only a malevolent Scrooge-like figure, mumbling over his glass of tap water in the corner, would dare to point out that if you are going to pore over a biochemistry textbook, and pick pathways out at random, then you can prove anything you like... And that's when you might start to think, well now, perhaps people who eat fresh fruit and vegetables are, just like the people who drink red wine in decorous moderation, living health-ily in all kinds of ways. Much like the people who buy vitamin pills. Lusty walks around country mansions. Cycling to work. That kind of thing.[3]

The article is flippant, but draws on a large body of research concerning not only the fuzziness of any conclusions about the real health effects of wine per se, but also the limita-tions of a style of evidence production that so many of us put great faith in without knowing much of anything about how it works. Goldacre's is a well-needed, if sure to go unheeded, intervention, as much so now as it was in 2007. One need only look to this Christmas headline from the Montreal newspaper *L'Express*: "Le vin rouge prévient du vieillissement, c'est scientifiquement prouvé" ("Red wine prevents aging, it's scientifically proven"), which cites an article from the journal *Nature* that turns out to have noth-ing specifically to do with red wine, or even with human beings.[4] While Goldacre's piece is more about marketing and bad science journalism (or science-indifferent health journalism), by ending on an implied note of *just drink it, goddammit*, he also hints at something that concerns me about this whole phenomenon.

That is, the normalization of a moral economy wherein such things as chocolate and wine need to be justified by their ostensible health benefits, as guilty pleasures redeemed, while the structure of spiritual blackmail remains perfectly intact. It is an economy wherein our health and the maintaining thereof take on a personal moral valence—the individual sits at the centre of a constellation of "lifestyle choices," and the story of their good works are believed to be writ on and in the body, like a modern-day vindication of *The Picture of Dorian Gray* (for the story was not so much about Gray being protected from aging by his painted proxy, but from the literal, corporeal degradation of his flesh that was thought to be the just and inevitable consequence of his depravity). If you will pardon my hyperbole, at its worst this facilitates the blaming of the disease-ridden poor for not exercising and for eating too many Junior Bacon Cheeseburgers, and at its less extreme it still constitutes the selling of our pleasures back to us as (health) virtues. That is a calculation I don't much care for. If you are going to drink and gourmandize and gorge, at least do so because it is the stuff of life, not because it is supposed to hold forth the promise—but not even the promise! Only a probabilistic, anonymous, statistical implication, an association!—of some extension of your otherwise miserable existence. Or, if you are going to lard yourself and your drinking in quasi-medical justifications, at least have the good aesthetic sense to go grander. Rustle up a rationale with a little more pizzazz: do so on the basis of old-wives' tales or epigrams from doomed novelists, humoral medicine, the doctrine of signatures, or just to keep your skeleton from jumping out your damn mouth in search of some less feeble flesh.

1 See www.AllTrials.net and www.OpenTrials.net, respectively, as well as Goldacre's "OpenTrials: Towards a Collaborative Open Database of All Available Information on Clinical Trials," *Trials* no. 17, 2016.

2 See A.P. Prayle, "Compliance with Mandatory Reporting of Clinical Trial Results on ClinicalTrials.gov: A Cross-Sectional Study," *BMJ* vol. 344, no. 7373, 2010.

3 Ben Goldacre, "Behold the Christmas Miracle of Antioxidents," *BMJ* vol. 335, no. 7630, 2007.

4 Joseph A. Baur et al., "Resveratol Improves Health and Survival of Mice on a High-Calorie Diet," *Nature*, November 2006.

On Natural Wine, Punk Rock,
and Too-Easy Analogies

Moving in wine circles, one often hears natural wine described as the "punk rock" of the wine world, whether in reference to individual *enfant-terrible* producers (such as Andrea Calek in Ardèche, or Collectif Anonyme in Banyuls) or to the prevailing anti-establishment ethos of a "movement" that, depending on whom you ask, may not actually exist as such. British booze writer Henry Jeffreys has been one of few to pursue this analogy with any specificity:

> Punk was a reaction against bloated prog rock or packaged pop like Olivia and John. It promised to return to the true spirit of rock 'n' roll. Natural wines are a reaction to over-manipulated wines made to impress rather than to drink. They hark back to some sort of prelapsarian past where wine was pure.[1]

Natural wine, the lack of an official definition notwithstanding, can be thought of as wine that is both more and less than organic: made by people, usually small vintners who grow their own grapes rather than buy them from farmers, who eschew chemical pesticides, fertilizers, additives, and other "corrective" interventions, both in the field and in the winery, but who may not participate in the regulatory apparatus of organic certification. Beyond this fairly cursory description, natural wine, like punk, can be understood as a threat against the established orders of taste and cultural production (and in the case of wine, even of agricultural production). Its provocation straddles the aesthetic and moral divide, wielding authenticity as a weapon in (potentially irrelevant) battles over what even deserves to be considered "wine." And, as is to be expected, there is an appropriate amount of vitriol and polemic to be found on both sides of the discussion. The colossally influential critic Robert Parker famously referred to natural wine as a "major scam being foisted on wine consumers,"[2] *Newsweek* dismissed it as tasting "worse than putrid cider,"[3] and in perhaps one of the most punk analogies to date, wine writer Stuart Pigott pointed to "so-called 'natural' wines, meaning wines that in the cellar where they were made were allowed to behave like badly brought-up teenagers who seldom wash or shave and ignore the everyday rules of polite behavior," as the crux of the problem with what he has described as the rise of the "hipster sommelier."[4] On the opposing front, natural wine advocates have dubbed the process of globalization and de-diversification of wine "Parkerization,"[5] and with such labels as "natural wine," "authentic wine," and "real wine," it is not difficult to imagine in what esteem they hold the rest of the wine world (often dismissed as "conventional" or "industrial" wine). The rhetoric of romantic radicalism runs strong, not least in the words of filmmaker and natural wine advocate Jonathan Nossiter, director of *Mondovino* (2004) and *Resistenza Naturale* (2014):

> In ten years, these renegades have transformed the basic idea of wine, especially in France and Italy, while exposing the cynicism and chemical manipulation of most conventional wine... These natural winemakers have scorned the cynical bureaucratic compromise of certified "organic" wine to renew a libation that has provided joy and comfort for eight thousand years.[6]

In short, one can discern a minor moral panic within the rarified confines of the wine world occasioned by this naturalist provocation that is not dissimilar to the aesthetic horror with which early punks were met (and in most small towns probably continue to be met, if my own experience as freaky teen in the mid-nineties means anything).

In his article, Jeffreys speculates as to whether the decline in relevance and appeal of punk rock also contains a lesson for us about the future of natural wine. After all, claims of music journalists aside, was not punk merely a trend fuelled by an able hype machine and the seductive allure of youthful iconoclasm, of which only a few credible scraps remain? Jeffreys writes,

> In my opinion, punk's influence is best heard in bands that took the spirit but not the music such as Dexy's Midnight Runners and the Pogues. But natural wine is surely also, like punk, clever marketing no matter how much the organisers of the various natural wine fairs try to deny it.

This is where I think Jeffreys' comparison falters—not on the grounds of the weakness of the analogy, but on his ultimate ignorance of his chosen analog. Like the majority of popular commentators on the history of punk, Jeffreys makes the mistake of conflating the demise of the phenomenon itself with the expiry of its time in the limelight. Only in recent years have music critics and wider audiences come to be vaguely aware that long after the Ramones and the Sex Pistols burned out or graduated to stadium shows and Spector Sound, there remained ever-growing legions of disaffected, irritated, impassioned youth who continued putting on concerts, piling into vans and releasing shitty, brilliant records (or, as often, tapes) for other shitty, brilliant kids. Where is the emergence of hardcore punk in Jeffreys' analogy, or Riot Grrrl? Or Ebullition Records and the publication of newsprint magazines like *Maximum Rock'n'Roll* and *HeartattaCk,* to say nothing of the uncountable thousands of DIY zines and labels? Where are Fugazi and Bikini Kill, Spitboy and His Hero Is Gone and Los Crudos in this narrative? They are invisible precisely because the account presumes the significance and the relevance of punk rock were coterminous with the attention paid to it by mainstream music journalism.

So what does a revised, better-informed understanding of punk's history (and present) contribute to such an analogy? While I don't disagree with Jeffreys' suggestion that "Time will tell which producers turn out to be the Boomtown Rats and which the Pogues," I think there is an interesting lesson about taste and appreciation to be considered. Perhaps one of the most valuable contributions of natural wine, on an intellectual and aesthetic level, may be to destabilize and encourage reconsideration of what it means to be a "good wine" (as punk did with the idea of a "good band"). While there are numerous natural wines that are excellent by even the most traditional standards, whether it be the turbidity of an unfiltered wine, a whiff of animal funk, or the slight spritz of latent fermentation in the bottle, many natural producers have helped to create a space for appreciating qualities otherwise proscribed as faults or flaws—new avenues for experiencing and making sense of the pleasures of drinking; like feedback and screaming, outside of the conventional register of taste.[7]

On a recent visit to Montreal, natural winemaker Olivier Lemasson commented that in France, for the most part, no one knows or cares who he is—there he is a farmer, it is only in Montreal and New York and London that he is treated like a rock star. Indeed, it is notable that much of the furor surrounding "natural wine" is to be found among the wine critics, sommeliers, and journalists, rather than the vintners themselves. So perhaps more important is what the story of punk rock suggests for the future of natural wine: the possibility that when the trend has subsided, there will nevertheless remain a community of committed producers and appreciators who continue to believe in the importance of a vibrant opposition to the standardized and soulless (or what they view as such). Toiling in relative obscurity and indifference to the market as the primary arbiter of taste, making what they love and loving what they make. DIY or die.

---

1 "Punk Rock Wine," Tim Atkin (blog), April 2, 2015.

2 *Wine Advocate*, 2010, p. 191.

3 Bruce Palling, "Why 'Natural' Wine Tastes Worse Than Putrid Cider," *Newsweek*, July 11, 2014.

4 "The Rise of the Hipster Somm, Part III: Awesome Hair and the Death of the Delicious," Grape Collective (blog), June 2016.

5 Alice Feiring, *The Battle for Wine and Love: or How I Saved the World from Parkerization* (Houghton Mifflin Harcourt, 2008).

6 Jonathan Nossiter, "Film and Wine in the New Dark Ages," *Film Quarterly*, vol. 67, issue 3, 2014.

7 For an expanded discussion of natural wine and so-called "orthodoxies of taste," see "Bad Melons, Bullshit, and the Emergent Qualities of Wine," in this volume.

Hot Dogs on the Brink of Insanity

Niagara Falls is a ghost town. Sort of. I mean, it feels like a ghost town. Which I guess is a strange thing to say about a bustling casino hot spot, except that the entire time we were there it all felt totally uncanny. The bus dropped us off, I have no idea where, but it was dark and still, and as far as we could tell, utterly abandoned. Off the main strip, certainly, but where was the main strip, even? One would assume that the promised storm of light and bustle would be discernible from miles off, but all that was palpable was the summer gloaming, murky and humid. It felt like the South, or stepping into Jim Jarmusch's *Mystery Train*. It felt like Lumberton.

We scraped together some pocket change to buy some ill-considered mix (something strawberry-kiwi that tasted like strawberry-battery) from the bus-station vending machine to soften the pints of cheap liquor we had earlier obtained, and set off in what seemed believably to be the direction of the water, the border, and, as we understood it, the Action. For a town built around millions of gallons of rushing water, it was surprisingly quiet. It felt like we would shortly meet an old derelict who would, with the ominous good nature of the insane, tell us, "Oh, casino? There used to be a casino round here, years back, the most majestic gambling house in all the land. Wasn't a vice or predilection the devil invented that couldn't be had, or at least sought, within those walls. Never closed, never slowed, shucks, no one ever got a wink of sleep until they plum collapsed, the times they had. But that was a long time ago, all gone now, gone since the [insert fire, locusts, murder spree, anything that would result in a torso heap]," and we would carry on until, out of the mist, a casino would rise.

Then something rose. A theme park? A tourist trap? Crowds, anyway. Screaming teenagers, muscleheads, loudly patterned shirts. Everyone stumbling or swaggering, or the strange elliptical herky-jerk that comes of trying to subordinate one to the other. Towns like this feel almost like what would happen if the carnival set up and just never left, but then instead of developing into some kind of (awesome) Lost Boys/Lankhmar/Foot Clan–style stronghold, it cleaned itself up a little, and the carnies got complacent and respectable and corrupt and started hosing down the sidewalks a little more regularly. None of it seemed quite right. Like it would all in the light of morning have vanished into the mist, returned to an empty centre, a ghost town haunted by a dream of its own shabby decadence. We spent a good chunk of the night, as far as I can tell, drinking Pabst and scheming in a bar featuring three screens playing MMA, surrounded by teenagers who looked like they must work and live there, because they certainly didn't give a fuck about the attractions. Beyond that, I hazily recall a lot of wax museums, some sort of race against time that involved doing several bourbon shots in a Boston Pizza that may also have been a video arcade, chasing or possibly being chased by a skunk in a vast field, and collectively dropping something like fifty dollars to ride a Ferris wheel that had little enclosed booths like a Zipper or gondola or I guess an enclosed Ferris wheel. And a lot of agitation about a "Frankenburger," which upon further examination turned out to just be the excess thrills and chills from Frankenstein's Haunted House spilling onto the roof of the Burger King next door, not an establishment itself, or an item available to be consumed. I suppose if one thinks about it, pretty much all burgers are Frankenburgers, to the extent that they are just amalgams of flesh from this and that unlucky animal.

Eight hours later: hell, we're all Frankenburgers.

A friend of mine acquired from her mother an expression that I rather like: "close to the veil." It could be that you are sick, or hungover, or just running low, but you begin to suspect that you are not far from that thin film that divides the living from the dead or, at the very least, life from non-life. If ever did two or three fuckers wake up feeling close to the veil, shrinking from the unforgiving light of the day star, we were they. No veisalgic bliss here. Just the kind of hangover where you wonder, "Is this what the dead feel like? Is this what a zombie feels like?" I think of *Return of the Living Dead*, where the cannibalistic fervour of the zombie is explained in terms of zombies being otherwise conscious, cognate human beings who are trapped in dead, creaking, decaying bodies. They can feel all the rot, the damage, the arrested, pooling blood, the worms that feed within, and in such a state they know that the only thing that will provide relief, however momentary, is brains. The hungover nincompoop has no such refuge in certainty. The hungover nincompoop has no brains to save him. At best, we spend our day in perilous, naive questing for the one food or drink that will compensate, will make us feel okay. We continue to stuff things into our already-ravaged bodies, increasing the workload of our beleaguered digestive system, weighing us down, weighting us for the grave.

Naturally, we thought an Italian-American Canadian Eatery would be the answer to our hangovers. Naturally, it was not. Just bad linguine and Bellinis and more lessons taught but unlearned. We thought back to the restaurant of the casino that we had eventually attained the night previous, sitting with two pints each of Molson Canadian in front of us because apparently even in Brigadoon they have last call. There had been a siren or alarm of some sort going off; no one had seemed especially concerned, but it didn't sound like a "winning" alarm. We were reminded of how sad and bleak and boring is the inside of a casino, and how none of us really knew how to gamble or, for that matter, had any money to gamble with. We certainly weren't feeling very lucky. And that is the story of the time I went to Niagara Falls and, against all odds, lived to tell about it. We didn't quadruple our money, but to our (dubious) credit, we didn't even try.

The Bellini, it does nothing.

Reflexes and Reflexions

"To cook something to exactly the right degree is a
delicate operation which requires great care, scientific
interest, and art—that is to say, love."
—Édouard de Pomiane[1]

While this goes against my actual cooking practice (non-
scientific interest, careless measurement, reckless abandon),
I like the idea of love as involving rigour—that it demands
something of they who love, and of the beloved. That however much our romantic mythos emphasizes the falling in and
the being swept away, there is something to love beyond or
irreducible to emotion or affect. Pomiane performs an interesting inversion here—not merely that love is an essential
ingredient in cooking, but that carefulness, scientific interest,
and art are themselves components of love. Can't trust love
to the heart alone, I might be tempted to say.

I've been reading the Modern Library's edition of
Cooking with Pomiane, skimming the recipes while relish-
ing Pomiane's style and personality, but I am annoyed to
discover how difficult it is to get clear information on the
source of the text. In her introduction, Ruth Reichl refers
to *Cooking with Pomiane* as the first of his books to be
published, in the 1930s, but when one actually looks at his
list of French publications, it is nowise clear of which of
these books it is a translation. I would like to believe that
it is *Réflexes et réflexions devant la nappe* (somewhat less
sonorously in English, *Reflexes and Reflections at Table*), as
that evokes the play of the involuntary and the intentionally introspective that runs through his work, although it
may be *Bien manger pour bien vivre* (*Better Eating for Better*

Living). It is my suspicion that *Cooking with Pomiane* is possibly an anthology. This, and the attendant difficulty of pinpointing when the text or texts were written, is unfortunate because many of Pomiane's *réflexions* concern the past: the past of French cuisine, and his own. It is the way in which his recipes are larded and barded with memoir that makes the book so attractive:

> These *friands* bring back all my childhood. Alas, the people I loved have vanished. Asphalt has covered the fields of the Butte Montmartre and the streams have disappeared beneath the pavements. (54)

But the book has come unmoored in time, and it is difficult to situate this nostalgia—is this the Pomiane of the 1960s or of the 1930s who is looking back so wistfully? Elsewhere, he writes:

> What would our lives be like without tradition? What terrible fatigue would overwhelm humanity if it only had to concern itself with the future? Tradition represents a momentary pause in the course of toil—repose and backward glance toward the past—the comparison of today with yesterday. Tradition is the memory of happy moments which have vanished, and their ephemeral return to life. (8)

This is certainly a rosy view of tradition, as that which rests and revives rather than stifles and binds, but Pomiane is considered neither reactionary nor conservative. He has been hailed by many as a culinary Modern, even an iconoclast, and has been cited as an intellectual forefather of molecular gastronomy by no less than the coiner of the term, Hervé This. Pomiane was himself a scientist and phy-sician and worked at the famed Pasteur Institute in Paris. I believe we can read in Pomiane the best of the spirit of molecular gastronomy (or the spirit of the best molecular gastronomy). The public face of molecular gastronomy is too often that of wild abstraction, deconstruction, or the technological colonization of the kitchen by a perhaps scientistic or mad-scientific rationality. But there is also a respect for tradition, and for the foods themselves, com-bined with an unwillingness to be bound by that tradition. One could say that molecular gastronomy is (the formal grounding of) the theory, which undertakes a demystifica-tion of the kitchen, while modern(ist) cooking is the practi-cal remystification of the cuisine.

To make explicit the connection, it is important to bear in mind Hervé This's point that molecular gastronomy is not a style of cooking, despite how the term is bandied about. Gastronomy is the study of food, cooking, and eating. It pertains to the production of a body of knowl-edge. Molecular gastronomy (or in its earlier, more accu-rate if more unwieldy formulation, "molecular and physical gastronomy") is thus about developing an understanding of food and cooking based specifically in the hard sci-ences. Modern/modernist cooking is about taking this understanding as a starting point and using not only the theoretical apparatus of chemistry and physics, but also its material battery (such as the infamous centrifuge) to take the preparation of food in new directions.

This distinction is important, and I find it makes the term "molecular gastronomy" that much less annoy-ing. So when Pomiane speaks of the art, science, and *love* involved in cooking food to exactly the right temperature, one can't help but have the thermal immersion circulator spring to mind. The thermal immersion circulator, as the name implies, is a device that maintains a meticulously constant temperature by way of a circulating water bath; it is a common piece of laboratory furniture. In the 1970s, it found a culinary application, allowing chefs to cook things slowly and evenly to extremely accurate temperatures, while reducing moisture and flavour loss by vacuum sealing. If anything exemplifies molecular gastronomy's reputation for cold abstraction, it is the Americanization of the French term *sous vide* as "cryovacking," but it is this care/careful attention that may be claimed to bridge the gulf between rigour and romance. It is the technological answer to Pomiane's heart's desire, or so I think its exponents would aver, perhaps going so far as to say that the thermal immersion circulator is a kind of cyborg technology of love, the love that must necessarily animate good cooking (no one would say that, actually). The use of this technology raises the question of whether such instruments are better thought of as shortcuts (the machine watches the pot so you don't have to) or as extensions of human capability—enabling a degree of care previously unavailable—or perhaps as a sort of technological precising definition of the act of love?

I had another worlds-collide moment when I read that while at the Pasteur Institute, Pomiane (or Édouard Pozerski, as he was known when not writing food lit) worked with Felix d'Herelle on his pioneering study of bacteriophage—a class of what were eventually decided to be viruses that feed specifically on bacteria and have been the source of much insight and confusion in the history of virology, and also an important early subject in the emergence of molecular biology as a scientific enterprise. Historically, molecular biology has been understood as developing out of the migration of physicists (and their wacky instruments) into life sciences research, specifically organic chemistry, and d'Herelle's Phage Group played a big part in this.[2] Just as molecular gastronomy reconfigures our culinary knowledge along chemical and physical lines, so too did molecular biology bring about a similar change in our understandings of life itself, by spinning out viral material into its component parts in the ultracentrifuge—another piece of laboratory equipment that has been borrowed by culinary modernists from physics, by way of organic chemistry, to now render possible all your favourite carotene foams and verbena caviar pearls. As such, Pomiane and This may be seen as figures in the same historical trajectory, bringing to bear chemical and physical ways of knowing first to the stuff, and now finally the staff, of life. How about that?

---

1 *Cooking with Pomiane* (Modern Library, 2001).

2 If by some freak chance you would like to know more, see Angela Creager, *The Life of A Virus: Tobacco Mosaic Virus as an Experimental Model, 1930-1965* (University of Chicago Press, 2002); and Ton van Helvoort, "What Is a Virus? The Case of Tobacco Mosaic Virus," *Studies in the History and Philosophy of Science* 22, no. 4 (1991), 557–588; and "The Construction of Bacteriophage as Bacterial Virus: Linking Endogenous and Exogenous Thought Styles," *Journal of the History of Biology* 27, no. 1 (1994a), 91–139.

God Won't Be the Wiser

If food magazines are good for anything, it is exposing one to bits of obscure culinary miscellany like oyster stout, or some new use for tangerine slices on raw pork chops, or the little dumplings in Swabian Maultaschensuppe. Swabia (or Schwaben) is an area of southern Germany often stereotypically derided for being full of *dummkopfs*, despite having produced Brecht, Einstein, Heidegger, and Herman Hesse, as well as some of the most elegant Spätburgunders going. The dumplings—*maultasche*—typically contain some combination of ground and smoked meat, spinach, and herbs in a pastry wrapping, and enjoy protected designation of origin (PDO) status within the EU, in doubtless more famous company with champagne, Parmigiano-Reggiano, Cornish pasties, and the like. The dumplings are also known as Herrgottsbescheißerle, or "little ones to cheat the lord." The name supposedly derived from the practice of monks in the Maulbronn monastery (Maulbronn's other claim to fame being that a young Hermann Hesse once tried to commit suicide there) "hiding" meat in pockets of dough during Lent on the rationale that it would disguise the act of rebellion from God.

It's an appealing story, but it has either been wildly exaggerated over time or those monks are totally awesome. Because really, if true, it is more than just funny, it is implicitly heretical—not only because it makes a total mockery of Lent, but because it contravenes the doctrine of divine omniscience, which is a pretty ballsy theological move to make just to *pretend* you're getting away with eating meat. I would argue that it has such an aura of the ridiculous that it is hard not to detect in it a note of spite, like Camus's "Il n'est pas de destin qui ne se surmonte par le mépris" ("There is no fate that cannot be surmounted by scorn"), or at least of irreverence—which, in this context, may be worse. And I suppose if we're accepting that He Who Created the Universe can't see beneath a paper-thin layer of dough, it's maybe not such a stretch to assume that He was in the can or something the entire time you were preparing the dish, and so didn't see you packing the meat in there in the first place. It conjures this image of a whole cloister of monks having a simultaneous crisis of faith, but rather than abandoning the ritual of study, prayer, and seclusion, they decide to spice up the routine by playing a sweet prank on God.

That it has to do with food is of obvious appeal for me, but I also just find it an immensely sympathetic sort of gesture, because, I mean, don't we all sometimes want to hide from God? Won't we join the monks someday, shrugging our shoulders, palms upturned in antic fashion as the hellfire licks and scorches our rascal chins?

Just a Lazy, Skull-Boiling Afternoon

I have been, as it were, fumbling toward butchery for many years now, since I in my late twenties saw my veganism washed away in a torrent of eggs and blood, and like so many sought to justify my return to carnivory by dint of a commitment to some version of "nose-to-tail" eating. Early in that process a couple of friends acquired a whole hog, and after much sweating and cursing and not inconsiderable toil on their part, we ended up with big old pig's head that demanded some doing with. We decided to have a crew of folks over and make an event of it, or to make a soup of it, and of the soup, make an event. We opted for an approximation of a Mexican *pozole*, which involved stewing the head for the better part of a day, stripping as much meat off the skull as possible, and to this adding chilies, achiote, tomatoes, and hominy, and finished it with avocado, cilantro, lime, cabbage, and tortillas. Bang: pig's head soup.

At the time I had only scant comfort with meat preparation, and I had never seen, handled, or eaten a pig's head. I really had no idea how I would cope. A pig's head, in case you are not aware, has eyes and eyelashes and teeth and a nose—all the makings of a face. And how does one face such a face, on a terrain of both recognition and consumption? For many a non-vegetarian, this remains an encounter one would prefer to avoid, lest it dispel the fantasy of the food animal as just a bunch of steaks taped together. But I, for one, was happy to be afforded the opportunity to face up to what was left of that particular face, despite it having been rendered somewhat more gruesome by being already de-jowled, for guanciale purposes.

As it turned out, I was able to approach the whole affair with alacrity, curiosity, and a measure of (perhaps necessarily?) irreverent humour. Certainly there were moments, whether we were wrenching out teeth to make jewellry, jabbing around the inside of the skull with a chopstick to free what was left of the brain matter from its cranial safety, or putting sunglasses on the head to snap photos, when we paused, as if awakened from some feverish meat dream, to ask ourselves, "Is this right? Are we going to hell? We're definitely going to hell." One person's immediate response to the "Cool Pig" photo op was along the lines of, "Oh, that is just wrong." But I wonder, wherein does the wrongness reside? Is "irreverent" even the best way to characterize it? And is this irreverence the same as a lack of reverence for life or, for that matter, for death?

On the one hand, I think irreverence is important. Humour is important; it can help us deal with the colossal misery and idiocy of the world, to put things into different perspective, to cope, and even to heal (of course, humour can as easily be hateful and hurtful, but I don't believe this nullifies its other potential). On the other, some kind of reverence for life seems necessary, but what do we mean when we talk about reverence for life? What do we assume about how reverence is experienced, and how it is expressed? Is it all hushed tones, deference, platitudes? This doesn't feel like quite the appropriate form—at least, not the only form—where food is concerned. And on the face of it (or beneath the skin of it), is this any different from playing with one's food? For it is indeed the face that arouses our moral sentiment, that challenges us to go beyond its status as food and react with disgust, empathy, horror. But then, we can say "beyond" food only if we have already accepted and normalized the separation of food from life, from lives.

Where in this chain of fragmentation, of transformation from an entity to an edible, does it become, or cease to be, in poor taste to play with one's food? To joke around with a head, rhyme and revel with the dead?

I don't have an answer. I believe there is some difference between a playful, productive irreverence and a problematic disrespect, but it is maybe one of those indefinable "I know it when I see it" distinctions. In the end, maybe the point is that it was about more than the head anyway, and maybe we erred by trying to understand the moral valence of the head in isolation. Do the sunglasses and selfies outweigh the homage of assembling a dozen-odd friends not only to share a delicious meal, but also to share an encounter with a challenging or unfamiliar cut of meat, and together come to understand just how much work one has to devote just to turn it into food? To see how it comes apart, is broken down? This was a challenge, and in its own way, a celebration. An homage to the pig that says not for squeamishness alone will any part be deemed unfit to eat. Thanks, Cool Guy.

La Langue Sans Visage

Butchery can be viewed as an exercise in abstraction; at least as concerns the transformation of whole, once-living animals into cuts of (especially muscle) meat that retain few traces of their original provenance and function. Cows and pigs, lamb and fish, into steaks and chops, and loins and filets. With the exception of offal, or so-called (with a certain flare for euphemism) "variety meats," which tend to persist in their corporeality and, for some people, speak too discernibly of the animal forms from which they were so rudely excised. For my own part, form is not so big an issue as taste. I, at one point in my life, made it something of a moral principle to not shrink from such items out of squeamishness, to make a test of the mettle of my nascent carnivory. I now am quite convinced that I can comfortably persist in my ethical cowardice no matter how many feet or faces I eat, so I am happy to explore unfamiliar bits and bobs and revisit those that I genuinely enjoy: hearts and bones, a bit of blood, for some reason tripe again and again, in spite of how frequently I am thwarted by it, and—enthusiastically if not that often—tongue.

Tongue salad. Why does the tongue seem to suggest itself so readily to the salad form? My first, a spicy Sichuan pork tongue with cucumber salad, was the most jarring. Not for its taste (for the tongue being a muscle is quite mild, meaty, and, in this case, dressed in chilies and coriander and black vinegar), but for its texture, combined with its very brazen identity as a tongue. I say now that form and anatomical frankness are no great deterrents, but we were all young once, and some of us vegan, even. Commonly, the preparation of tongue calls for boiling, followed by peeling to render it more (ahem) palatable. This tongue, however, was unpeeled, and quite covered with taste buds. Big ones, some of them. Thus, one was presented with the somewhat unsettling experience of taking into one's mouth and chewing something very hauntingly reminiscent—in both surface texture and structural resistance—of the experience of accidentally biting down on one's own tongue.

Not lessened by its impossibility, I couldn't help when my taste buds brushed against structures so similar, imagining the tongue continuing to taste even as it was mashed into non-existence, picturing some ghost-pig tasting me from beyond the grave by sheer habitual force of spirit on the part of the organ. And who better positioned to haunt than the food-animal, denied a proper resting place by the fragmentation and dispersal of being made meat (anthropologists call this faunal processing), then still further by digestion, partial incorporation, and defecation; then subject to the final indignity of disintegration amidst the sewage. No grave, no eulogy, no funeral.

The second, a Russian salad of chopped beef tongue, pickles and mayonnaise, possibly hard-boiled eggs. Consumed in a basement restaurant in Côte-des-Neiges (a neighbourhood that has the honour of being on "the other side of the mountain" from just about any other neighbourhood in Montreal), decorated in fake stone and stuffed (taxidermied) animals, served with a crystal phial of ice-cold vodka. The dish translated as "mother-in-law's-tongue salad" in I don't know whether a venerative or vengeful specimen of Caucasian wit. More recently, I ate a warm salad of bison tongue with tarragon, which was certainly the most delicately prepared of these three. It elicited in my dining companion a reaction reminiscent of, but quite dissimilar to, my first encounter with the pig's tongue. Where I was struck by weird supernatural and autophagous associations, she was shocked by the voluptuous sensuality of the tongue—hers was a living tongue, a loving tongue. The look on her face, accompanied by a quick blush, was as if she had committed a public indiscretion. If there was a ghostly presence, it was more Patrick Swayze than Pet Sematary. Impressive all the more for a tongue that, unpeeled and still attached to its beast could, as she put it then, "lick the paint off a post."

Notes Preliminary to Actually Thinking about an Anti-Colonial Food Writing

In the autumn of 2014, I spent a month in Turkey. Travelling with a Turkish expat friend, we started in Istanbul, journeyed south to Göreme in the central province of Nevşehir, then west to the coast of the Aegean to visit her family home, cat, and quince trees in a tiny town called Çeşmealti. In the months, now years, that followed, I found it very difficult to begin to write about the trip. As one should imagine, it was not for the lack of material—my entire time there was one of almost uninterrupted culinary richness, from tart, thick-skinned yogourt to sweating glass chambers of steamed hamburgers on Taksim Square, incredible lamb *cağ kebabı* to incredibly tripey *kokoreç* off the street, ayran every day, tea every hour, spicy pickled turnip juice, lamb omelette in Urla, eating stuffed mussels on the street corner and oranges from Elif's parents' backyard one hundred feet from the saltiest sea that has ever had me, mint and freshly hulled pinto beans, olives, mint, olives, mint, more yogourt, cucumbers, wine made from grapes with names so laden with umlauts that I could not bear the mortification of attempting and failing to pronounce them. Listening to Bolt Thrower and Goat Horn in a bathroom-sized metal bar inBeyoğlu. Watching Bergman on a laptop, drunk in a cave hotel in Cappadocia. Seeking, but being too ill-prepared to know where to look for, some trace of James Baldwin's life in Istanbul four decades ago.

But I don't I know how to tell these stories—or how to tell them responsibly—to relate the experiences without succumbing to the sly, earnest, dishonourable exoticism of so much cultural tourism. There is, at best, a perverse self-consciousness at work in the minds of the usually white, usually anti-touristic cultural tourists as they move through an unfamiliar landscape attempting, as unobtrusively as possible, to find meals defined to a greater or lesser extent by their authenticity (even, as discussed earlier, their highly contingent, local, and multiple authenticity), experience them, and subsequently celebrate them (also as respectfully as possible) in their book/blog/travelogue of whatever persuasion. How does one convey the excitement of the unfamiliar respectfully and without lapsing into caricature when one has only the limited palette of the outsider with which to render it? Or conversely, how does one avoid the eating-of-the-other, the appropriation into which the insider or quasi-expert can so unintentionally slide? It is sometimes difficult to know how to dig oneself out of this quagmire of still quite narcissistic, if well-meaning, ethical/aesthetic paralysis.

It calls to mind, in a roundabout way, the furor generated a few years back by Adam Gollner's unfortunately-titled *Globe and Mail* article, "Why You Should Eat in Parc Ex, Montreal's Ungentrified Food Paradise,"[1] and the inevitable response published only days later in *Maisonneuve* magazine, which called Gollner out for pulling a "cultural gentrifier's hat trick" by "blending Orientalist generalizations, frontier-colonialist mentality and ironic detachment in order to obfuscate the structural violence of daily life in the neighbourhood."[2] The question of gentrification is slightly to the side of my main concern here, albeit an extremely important and salient one for food writing that is rarely addressed with sufficient nuance.[3] What struck me was more a matter of style and, I suppose, the politics thereof. Gollner has written ably and with inspiration and rigour about everything from Hungarian wine to the Arab underpinnings of Sicilian cuisine, fruit-smuggling to the quest for literal immortality.[4] "Why You Should Eat in Park Ex" served as a reminder of how easy it is for even a very accomplished writer to slip into a discourse of exoticization when writing about the food of "other" cultures—at least when one is attempting to write with some literary sensibility that extends beyond dry reportage.

Notions of wildness, of pre- or contra-modernity, noble suffering, or uninhibited celebration, even or especially of authenticity, all have their place in the elaborate discursive architectures of colonialism and Orientalism, and in their contemporary iterations. One may think of these as literary technologies—narrative, discursive technologies—for fixing Otherness in a fictional alterity (or fixing alterity as a fictional Otherness?) for our consumption. Now, we may debate the "real" impact of such symbolic violence, and the extent to which Western cultural analysis itself reproduces the silencing and dispossession of the "other" in whose defence it presumes to speak when it presents Orientalism as a totalizing discourse, but for the moment I want to keep things a little more reined in.

It suffices as a reminder of how accessible and salient are such colonial tropes for (especially white) authors writing within a Western literary tradition—perhaps all the more so for food writing, which is always balanced precariously between fluff, formal blandness, and something that occasionally pretends to literary merit, and so is especially susceptible to hackneyed sentiment and cliché, yet all the while dealing with something quite intimate and fundamental to survival and pleasure both (as much as I like to use food mostly as a vehicle for jokes and self-loathing). The challenge, then, is how not to fall into this trap when such tropes are so ready to hand for the making sense, and indeed the structuring, of our encounters with difference?

There is, of course, a risk in using these terms—colonial-ism, Orientalism—too freely, thus blunting their critical edge and the specificity of the histories and relationships that subtend them. The relationship between Canada and Turkey, for instance, is not a colonial one. Istanbul is not Urla is not Göreme, let alone Erzurum, Antep, et cetera. Colonialism and Orientalism cannot be reduced to one another. Nevertheless, with Turkey a predominantly Islamic country and Istanbul the smoky jewel of the West-ern imagination for about the last fifteen hundred years (arguably since there has been a West), it should not be a stretch for me to feel colonial and Orientalist tropes remain as major structuring elements for any attempt to produce a literary account of my experience there. Hell, the very books that opened my eyes to the possibilities of travel writ-ing were Patrick Leigh Fermor's *A Time of Gifts* and *Between the Woods and the Water*, which relate his youthful exploits en route by foot from "the hook of Holland to Constanti-nople" on the eve of the Second World War. And I have read far too much W. Somerset Maugham and Graham Greene to emerge untainted by the aesthetics of colonial nostalgia.

There is another dimension of this discussion that has less to do with Turkey or Parc Ex specifically and more to do with the colonial history of Canada itself. Lisa Heldke, a phi-losopher and food studies scholar, has used the term "food adventurer" to describe the kind of (mostly intra-national) culinary cultural tourism evoked by Gollner's article. She has her own ideas about "strategic authenticities" that at several points dovetail with my own, and her book *Exotic Appetites: Ruminations of a Food Adventurer* is devoted to navigating these issues as an aspiring "anticolonialist eater." In doing so, Heldke arrives at a sort of modified localist, sustainable agriculture-focused notion of "foodshed fidelity," which attempts to evade the essentialism and occasional xeno-phobia of such approaches by way of temporal and cultural pluralism. "In short," she writes, "I think the sustainable agriculture movement already stands in a position to give adventuring anticolonialists the opportunity to forge the kind of deep, significant links to our food that many of us have been seeking in our ethnic food forays."[5] Conspicu-ously absent from this formulation is any acknowledgement of the fact that agriculture in the U.S. and Canada, however sustainable, is intimately bound up with the history of set-tler colonialism, the seizure of First Nations and Native American land, and the Occidental terraforming project that underpins the two countries' existence. Although in her later work Heldke attempts to move away from the binary of local-ism versus cosmopolitanism, Native and First Peoples are all but erased in her account of "anticolonialist" eating, just as they are similarly absent from much of the discourse around localism and foraging in North America, that is, when they are not serving as fodder for appropriation by probably well-meaning foodies and restaurateurs. That's pretty bad.

If an anticolonial food writing is already a daunting pros-pect, that of a decolonizing food-writing practice seems positively overwhelming. The mythologies, symbolic registers, and material institutions that perpetuate these dynamics are substantial. They are ubiquitous, perhaps not inevitable, but they will not be evaded, let alone dismantled, without some imagination, humility, and force of will. I do not flatter myself that I am possessed of that imagination, or that honesty. But it's something to work on.

---

1 *Globe and Mail*, April 2, 2013.

2 Fred Burrill, "Orientalism, Gentrification and Irony in Parx Ex: A Response to the Globe and Mail," *Maisonneuve*, April 6, 2013.

3 The title of the accompanying photo gallery, which I don't expect was Gollner's doing, reads: "Montreal's Park Ex, an edgy hidden gem ripe for gentrification." Parc Ex is indeed on the cusp of gentrification, as the much-vaunted cheap rents of Montreal move ever north from the centre of the city, and with them the hipsters and artists and so on who serve as the (usually, hopefully) unwilling vanguard or sturmtruppen (in the WWI sense) of the process. Gentrification is of course a complicated social and economic process that indeed sometimes does involve the improvement of municipal infrastructure and economic revitalization its champions promise, albeit usually at the expense of its previous inhabitants being pushed out by rising rents. We may debate the relative "badness" of seeking out far-flung neighbourhoods in which to dine on the best (ethnic) _____ that is otherwise invisible in the culinary cartography of a city, but there is no denying the role that food writing/blogging plays in rendering such entire neighbourhoods more visible, attractive, and hence viable for predatory development. Is it a small role? Maybe. For my own part, as a white, middle-class resident of Parc Ex who is neither a Montreal native nor member of any of the communities—Italian, Greek, Indian, Pakistani, Bangladeshi, to a lesser extent Haitian—that have defined and continue to define the neighbourhood, I am of course implicated in this process, and I have no intention of trying to talk my way out of. So far the least conflicted actions I have come up with are shopping at the neighbourhood markets and not geo-tagging my Instagram posts. I'm basically a hero.

4 See "Hungary's Forgotten Wine Region Is Finally Getting the Respect it Deserves," *Saveur*, January 7, 2016; "Eating the Arab Roots of Sicilian Cuisine," *Saveur*, March 17, 2016; *The Fruit Hunters*, (Random House, 2009); *The Book of Immortality: The Science, Belief, and Magic Behind Living Forever* (Scribner, 2013).

5 *Exotic Appetites* (Routledge, 2003), 206.

Putting Yourself on the Line

There is always a gamble in having someone taste something you dearly love, that you think is one of the best
things you've ever tasted, for fear that in their failure to
enjoy it, some thread of sympathy, of connection, will be
foreclosed. It is like the fear of too strongly recommending
a book, lest the other person does not appreciate it, and in
so doing reveals the limits of their understanding of you,
or you they. I mean, it is not a great fear, but it sometimes
gives me pause.

Tastes are so idiosyncratic and so personal that to share a
taste for something can feel like a particularly strong form
of connection, and its lack all the more tragic. I wonder
if this is a risk that lies behind all sharing of food—that
while it is the basis of an important bond, "breaking bread"
together does not guarantee that bond but rather provides
the conditions of its possibility and, equally, its foreclosure.
I find there is a strange disconnect in cooking for others if
the food I have made makes others happier than it does
myself, or when someone thinks excellent what I consider
only adequate. The whole matter of one being one's own
worst critic is somewhat beside the point. I sometimes feel
it is a greater compliment when someone likes something
I've made only as much, roughly, as do I, when they can say,
"Yeah, this is pretty solid, I can see what you mean about
something being missing, but I wouldn't worry about it,"
rather than when they are moved to gush and/or rave.

Is that a selfish thing? Prizing one's own evaluations over
the happiness of others? A chilling thought, if one thinks
of cooking as an act of love, as it is often framed (counter-

posed against cooking as a self-aggrandizing and masculine exercise in technical mastery), but nevertheless I can see where I'm coming from (duh). In that shared critical evaluation—not identical to, but not utterly different from, a shared love—there is the consonance of something that makes sense to one making sense to another, so that one does not feel alone in it.

Gripping, Griping, a Derangement of the Bowels, a Vulture, or Griffin

I have said before, perhaps too often and too glibly, that I live my life in avoidance of the stomach ache, however little I modify my behaviour to the achievement of this end in practice, aside from excluding expired meat and psychedelic mushrooms from my diet. It is too fearsome; it suffuses and poisons the being, wrenches the soul a little from its seat (or wrenches the seat and so jars the soul), and makes an enemy of the whole world. One can enjoy nothing with a stomach ache.[1]

On my last trip to Mexico I had much occasion to think on and about dyspepsia, as gastrointestinal distress-verging-on-terror proved to be a nigh-constant companion. *This trouble*, I thought, *it loves me*. It walks beside me, to chide me, perhaps to guide me. From an uneasy bloat, perpetual and inconsistent with one's recent consumption, to the weakness, tremor, and indisposition of diarrhea,[2] to a general exhaustion and hyper vigilance for anything that might seek to liberate itself, under pretense of gas from the rosy confines of the gut. I wonder at the word itself. Dyspepsia, it turns out, is no common stomach ache, but the medicalization of indigestion, if you will. Derangement of the bowels, pain upon palpation, that sort of thing. It also has the dubious honour of being for me a word around which has collected thickly the coagula of memory, more viscous for it being the memory of embarrassment. By this I do not mean an embarrassing memory of dyspepsia itself (for who among us has not eaten a kilogram of dried apricots at some time or another, or a befouled country ham?), but of the very word, *dyspepsia*.

I cannot recall the grade (sixth?), but I remember the desk at which it was written, in the back room of my parents' house: a story for school about an invasion of small, crab-like aliens. Seeking a word to convey some fear, horror, trepidation or somesuch, I alighted with the aid of a thesaurus upon *dyspepsia*, which I took at face value as an appropriate synonym. However, I was later called out by my teacher for failing to realize that the word actually meant indigestion. I do not recall the context of the embarrassment. Was it a private humiliation? One performed in the margin notes and felt in the cleft between reader and text? I can't imagine it was a public shaming; I should remember such an event. But I do remember it as an early taste of shame of that sort: the stark not-knowing-of-a-word, finding myself exposed by either my own overreaching or the misapprehension by another of the extent of my knowledge. The second time, many years later, was with a university professor who called on me quite unexpectedly to apprise the rest of the class of the meaning of *bathetic*. Of which I had no idea, but you'd best believe have since made a point of remembering (for all the never that I am called upon to demonstrate it[3]). The third occurred while buying a boxing skeleton pen in a New York City bodega; it was revealed that I had been mispronouncing the word *chimera* all my life (the 1979 edition of the *Advanced Dungeons & Dragons Monster Manual* did not include pronunciations, alas). You get the idea. But *dyspepsia* came first.

There's a funny biographical recursion to this: the child known for his precocious vocabulary, shown up by its inadequacy, mortified by its and his failure, by the cipher of dyspepsia. Years later, the adult, known for his food fixation, makes a maxim of his desire to avoid at all costs the upset stomach. The same adult who never knows quite how to answer the question "Where does your interest in words come from?" Perhaps, after all, I am just trying to avoid dyspepsia.

---

1 It is with no shame (or at least, no shame distinguishable from or in excess of that which hums, ambient throughout my entire life) that I count among my long list of sexual failures that time I ate too much scotch and ribs and "had a tummy ache."

2 Diarrhea is also pretty interesting. Perhaps because, like vomiting, it is one of those rare experiences (rarer for non-menstruating types, I suppose) of a total lack of control over the body, an alienation from the flesh at the moment of its greatest excess (see Mary Douglas's 1966 *Purity and Danger: An Analysis of Concepts of Pollution and Taboo* for a canonical anthropological investigation of such "matter out of place"). One really does feel invaded in a way, or impregnated, become host to a stomach that has turned against the rest of the organism. Although I suppose in many (bacterial, parasitic) cases it is more a matter of the digestive tract taking extreme measures to expel some other unwelcome presence. "A disorder consisting of too frequent evacuation of too fluid feces," states the *OED*, "sometimes attended with griping pains." Would you believe that the entries for *gripe* and *griping* span two full pages? It is all "grasping," "gripping," "clutching tenaciously," "that which can be held in a hand," "spasms of pain, pangs of grief or affliction... An intermittent spasmodic pain in the lower bowls." Or—and it is for these archaisms that I love the *Oxford English Dictionary* —"a vulture, or griffin."

3 The sense in which I originally understood *bathos* pertained to a false or exaggerated heightening of emotion. However, this only captures part of its meaning. The *OED* gives it as "Ludicrous descent from the elevated to the commonplace, in writing or speech." The sudden slide from the sublime to the vulgar, which may be unintentional, as evidence of superficiality of affect or writerly ineptitude; or intentional, for comedic effect. In this respect, it may be even more significant a word than *dyspepsia* where my writing life is concerned. I leave it to the reader to decide whether to take it as intentional or not.

Across the Great Divide: Decentring the Organism and the Ontological Hangover

Hangovers are funny things. Funny in all of the usual laughingly lamentable, mind-stripped-bare-by-its-bachelors, wallowing-in-freakish-misery sorts of ways, but also in how they present an opportunity for uncontrolled experimentation with ways of feeling—ways of feeling *badly*, yes, but ways that sometimes open up new planes of badness, ways of being a body that foreground one's corporeality with terrific and (if we're lucky) fascinating immediacy. Kingsley Amis so adroitly gave us the notion of the metaphysical hangover,[1] and I have elsewhere written of my own experiences with the sublime hangover;[2] here, I would like to talk about what I call the ontological hangover.

I have been afforded the opportunity to explore this phenomenon, I believe, as the result of my perhaps too-avid appreciation for wild-fermented beers and, to a somewhat lesser extent, so-called natural wines. One of the more exciting turns the international craft beer world has taken in recent years is the renewed interest in wild and indigenous yeasts, spontaneous fermentation, and experiments with barrel aging. Most of which is owed to the Belgian tradition, for while we have Pasteur to thank for elaborating the mechanics of open fermentation and laying to rest the idea of spontaneous generation (and ironically, in the process spontaneously generating a world of microbes around us[3]), pre-Belgian Low Countrymen had been fermenting beer in open vats, aging them in empty wine barrels, and letting all sorts of weird-ass bacteria get involved since the 1500s.[4] Now we have all sorts of craft breweries eager to experiment with the old traditions, combining a venerative and curatorial spirit with an almost postmodern iconoclasm (from traditional breweries like Cantillon, Drei Fonteinen, and Boon to newer players like Mikkeller, Crooked Stave, and Le Castor, among others), and coming out with some fantastic beers. It may be pure biophilia (or biofetishism?) to say that these beers taste especially "lively" as a result of their greater microbial diversity (such beers are produced interdependently by pediacoccus, lactobacillus, and various brettanomyces strains as much as by the more common saccharomyces yeasts), because it already takes a certain orientation toward the messiness of life for descriptions like lactic acid, horse blankets, and farmyard to come off as lively as opposed to, say, fetid, in an aromatics context. But blast, I possess such an orientation, and these beers have such a taste.

Now, I realize that there are some very important differences between such beers and natural wines: many modern breweries still inoculate their ferments with selected "wild" yeasts or yeasts harvested from fruits or infected barrels, rather than allowing fermentation to occur in tanks open to the vagaries of the air (the awesomely named Flemish *koelship* or "coolship"), whereas natural winemakers rely solely on indigenous yeasts already present on the grapes. So, although it could be argued that winemakers tend to accord more importance to a sort of "microbial agency," what these products share is an engagement with the microbiopolitical world of yeasts and bacteria that differs significantly from the drinks to which many of us are accustomed (and certainly from distilled spirits, which have all such life stripped from them). They often exhibit considerable microbial diversity, which is to say that they, in some cases, are quite literally teeming with life, and they often taste super fuckin' weird. Weird and cool, refreshing or arresting, even, as I suggest above, vital.

I have often heard it claimed that natural wine does not give you a hangover. I will grant that compared to other wines one might drink, whether crummy corner-store poison or overblown, over-oaked, reverse-osmosed, and micro-oxygenated haut-plonk, more-or-less natural wines in equivalent quantities produce less brutal hangovers. I have never heard a similar claim made for wild beers, thankfully, for to suggest no hangover is a scandalous misrepresentation that actually does disservice to the singularity of the hangovers one can experience.

This hangover is perhaps best described as waking up with the immediate feeling of a balance having been tipped, as if your body is not poisoned but *occupied*—become home and host to the microflora of wherever, Vichte and the Zenne, Anchorage or Greensboro Bend. There is a taste that seems not so much to linger in your mouth as to be produced in your very saliva; it reminds you of all that you have taken in, drink upon drink, and inspires the suspicion that some perverse innovation in the typical food-to-energy equation might have been achieved, like an internal ferment has begun that might finally coax the self-identity of the flesh out of its jingoistic discretion. It reminds one that, as essential as the notion of the bounded self is to our day-to-day existence, our own organismic unity is something of a phantasm. The human genome is already as much as 8 percent composed of inherited endogenous retrovirus, which is to say viral material that sometime in the course of human evolution infected this or that person, and instead of being stomped by the immune system, incorporated itself into the germ line, in time undergoing sufficient mutations that the body ceased to realize that it wasn't part of the organism in the first place. Although now and then such proviruses seem to spontaneously regain their pathological bellicosity (a rare occurrence in humans, although there is research to suggest possible links between human endogenous retroviruses and forms of cancer and autoimmune disease), they are also believed to be involved in some essential life-perpetuating processes.[5]

Similarly, the Human Microbiome Project, which has set out to sequence, catalogue and comprehend the microbial makeup of the human body, has suggested that bacterial cells may outnumber our own cells by as many as ten to one. Even if more recent research has suggested this proportion may be more like 1:1 or 1:1.3, that still works out to our being (in DNA terms) as much "them" as "us."[6] Which to me suggests that some reconceptualization of that us-them schema demands consideration. Beyond matters of quantity and the essential role of gut microflora in our ability to digest and thrive off food, philosophies of embodied cognition have been delivered a conceptual kick in the pants of late by work indicating that these micro-organisms may also play a role in mood and mental health.[7] If we are already at the point of speculating that the enteric nervous system might operate as a sort of "second brain," then what of our clinging obsession to self-identity as a first principle? How do we think this body multiple? Perhaps we have never been (purely) human? Perhaps we have never been whole.

Such are the thoughts that occupied me, sitting on a stool in the dim of a carefully appointed New York gin bar one evening, where after days of deep immersion in the wilds of beer and wine I had begun to feel as if the tastes were tasting *me*. Following a succession of appropriately medicinal gins and bitters, in an attempt to scour my insides and supplant the ontological hangover with the more familiar and (conceptually) unchallenging regular hangover, I was feeling so much less yeasty and discombobulated; indeed, I was feeling so merely human that I could have sung a song, or kicked a cop. But even this semblance of order so precariously reattained, I couldn't shake the still-ambiguous lesson—or was it less a lesson than a question?—presented by the ontological hangover. Certainly, I felt fucked up, but was it so bad because I felt physically bad, or just so physically foreign to myself? That perhaps, contrary to the picture that biological individualism has painted for me, with such clean lines, contours well-defined, I am yet a collage of unaccounted-for brush strokes?

---

1 *Everyday Drinking* (Bloomsbury, 2008).

2 *Food and Trembling* (Invisible, 2011).

3 In his 1984 *The Pasteurization of France* (*Les Microbes: guerre et paix*) (Harvard), Bruno Latour explores how Pasteur over the course of his nineteenth-century research on fermentation, spoilage, and infection, effectively changed our sense of what entities make up the world. Before Pasteur's 1864 experiments, Latour claims, microbes simply did not exist. After 1864, however, they had always been there. For more elaboration on this notion, see basically Latour's entire bibliography, perhaps especially "On the Partial Existence of Existing and Nonexisting Objects" in Lorraine Daston's *Biographies of Scientific Objects* (University of Chicago Press, 1996); and *Pandora's Hope: Essays on the Reality of Science Studies* (Harvard, 1999).

4 For a very readable and informative tour through the history and techniques of wild fermented beer, see Jeff Sparrow's *Wild Brews: Beer Beyond the Influence of Brewer's Yeast* (Brewers Publications, 2005).

5 See Bhardwaj, N., & Coffin, John M. (2014). "Endogenous Retroviruses and Human Cancer: Is There Anything to the Rumors?" *Cell Host & Microbe*, 15(3), 255–259; Macfarlan, T. S. et al. (2012). "Embryonic Stem Cell Potency Fluctuates with Endogenous Retrovirus Activity," *Nature*, 487(7405), 57–63; Tugnet, N. et al. (2013). "Human Endogenous Retroviruses (HERVs) and Autoimmune Rheumatic Disease: Is There a Link?" *The Open Rheumatology Journal*, 7, 13–21.

6 See the Public Library of Science (PLoS) Human Microbiome Project collection at http://collections.plos.org/hmp.

7 See Bravo, J. A., Cryan, J. F. et al. (2011), "Ingestion of Lactobacillus Strain Regulates Emotional Behavior and Central GABA Receptor Expression in a Mouse Via the Vagus Nerve," *Proceedings of the National Academy of Sciences* U S A, 108(38); and Coghlan, A. "Gut Bacteria Spotted Eating Brain Chemicals for the First Time," *New Scientist*, July 21, 2016.

Flight from Reno

Only figuratively, not literally, a flight: the first Greyhound trip longer than two but shorter than seventy hours I have taken in over a decade. It's not so bad, save for the wacky-shack suspension of the vehicle and apparent recklessness of our driver. I don't believe she has slackened speed for a single ramp, off or on, and we are left with the feeling of teetering terrifically, as if on an antique roller coaster, perilously, seat beltlessly, hurtling ever forward. Also, we almost hit a transport truck. No big deal. The eighth-grader beside me asks, "Have you ever shot a real gun?" and proudly unfurls for me the poster-sized target of Osama Bin Laden that he has at some prior date dutifully riddled with bullet holes, and now carries rolled up with his carry-on. It is more charming than it sounds. He's bussing from Reno to Seattle, wants to play college basketball, and I notice by discreet glances at his iPod that he has been listening to a lot of Boys II Men.

I had been in Reno for three days to interview some scientists (long story). I learned a few things, kicked a piece of cactus, ate at a pizza place called Pie Face (had a highly alliterative but not unpleasant slice topped with pecorino, peas, and prosciutto, maybe?), and tasted country gravy for the first time. The gravy was part of a rather liberal riff on a plate of eggs Benedict, a hot, heavy brick of a breakfast for a hot, dry, desert day. The server congratulated me with a rough jocularity for not getting it all over my face, for which I had in silence already been congratulating myself, but I appreciated the recognition. It was a nice breakfast.

There are moments in life when one gets the feeling that the pace of things is being artificially interrupted, that by one's actions one is somehow moving just out of step with what should be the natural tempo, producing a hiccup in an otherwise well-described arc. Sitting curbside in front of the Reno bus station, I found myself wondering whether I shouldn't have taken a later bus. It would be a difference of only a couple of hours, but what could I have made of them? Barely had I wrapped up the business that brought me to Reno and I was hotfooting it out of town. I couldn't shake the feeling I was rushing something, missing something. I could take another bus, sit down, and dangle my feet in the river that I had only just discovered. Everybody uses the river as a reference point in Reno, and somehow it hadn't occurred to me earlier to go take a look. It's safe enough to swim in; people are swimming in it right now, I thought, right in the middle of town. I could have splashed around for a half-hour in a river in goddamn Reno while on my working vacation, chatted with the barista at Java Jungle, next to what I can only assume is its sororal wine bar, Jungle Vino, maybe had a mojito with that nurse I met on the way back from the university.

They have a twenty-five-cent Ms. Pac-Man machine in the Reno bus station, and though I marvelled at the anachronism, even if I didn't already have a marked disinterest in Pac-Man (Mr. or Ms.), I was warned away by the advice of a surly child—"Don't put money in, these machines are a crook. They're busted. I'm looking for the number so I can call someone."

I comforted myself, a coward's comfort, with my old maxim from a more transient time: it is better to leave a place feeling like you shouldn't. Better to leave a place wistful, so it can live a little life in your mind, rather than drag yourself out with the sickening feeling that you have stayed too long. But this amounts to what? Enshrining in a general principle that it is better to regret something you didn't do than something you did? Better to keep something alive as a dream, a fiction, a fond remembrance, than potentially ruin it by actually seeing it through? Better the one that got away? It is a rationalization made for gazing out a bus window, but that is some cold shit.

Whatever, Reno was dry. Reno was making my nose bleed.

The Timber by Which It Is Broken

Autumn of 2011 found me in a frenzy of brow-furrowing, pencil-tapping, and squinting off into the distance as I attempted to come up with a submission for the Oxford Symposium on Food and Cookery's *Wrapped & Stuffed* series. The deadline passed, of course (I perform poorly under pressure), and equally predictably, what fell into my lap not two months later but a nigh-perfect offering in the form of the "pickerel taco," on offer at a Toronto restaurant called Bannock. The quotation marks here are pointed, as the dish consists of "pickerel taco, on a steamed bun, w/ caviar tartar and cucumber-apple salad." Perhaps we are all now so saturated with the polymorphous perversity of menu nomenclature, and tacos, steamed buns (*bao*), banh mi endlessly interpenetrating in an orgy of referentiality, that such an object would pass unremarked in 2016, but in early 2012 it seemed too perfect to not excite comment.

I admit my first reaction was to just be like, "Shut up, Bannock." But, with the benefit of a few minutes' quiet reflection, it seemed what immediate offence I took merited further examination. What dire transgression does the pickerel taco represent? Is it merely the crass modishness of food culture, or the intellectual offensiveness of what I perceived as a category mistake (i.e.: "That is not a taco; where do you get off?")? A sort of conceptual disgust? But does such conceptual disgust not hinge on the presumption of conceptual—even cultural—purity, and is there not something of the conservative about such a response? A reaction to a perceived threat against a certain order that makes the hybrid monstrous, as opposed to merely mixed? Disgust—even of a conceptual as opposed to visceral sort—is a tricky bit of affect in that it tends to pass itself off as pre-political, in the process eclipsing a more thoughtful analysis of its object (even while inciting an almost fetishistic fixation thereupon), and what may be at stake in such consideration.

Concerning such questions as "Why call it a taco? What are they trying to prove?" the less charitable response is that Bannock is merely cashing in on the current popularity of the taco. Even if its star is no longer in ascendance, we are still living in Taco Time. They pop up in the most unexpected places. Everybody does a taco, or some reimagining thereof, whether to put their authorial imprint on the thing or simply to otherwise "rescue" it from the barrio. *Taco* is a word with very good culinary capital, whether or not what comes out on the plate bears much resemblance to a taco in the traditional sense. Further, while *fusion* as a word is fully out of vogue in culinary circles, Japanese/Chinese/Korean/ South-Asian "inspirations" and "inflections" abound, the Korean taco in particular being first to blow up (time will tell if kimchi is destined to be the new chipotle/roasted red pepper/sundried tomato), and the pickerel taco gets to mobilize both associations under the auspices of "Canadian Comfort Food."

Having now invoked tacos in the traditional sense, it is perhaps necessary to pause and offer some caveats. Talking about what is "traditional" or, still more charged, "authentically traditional," is always tricky because there is a tendency to represent the traditional as given, eliding both the internal difference and diversity of traditional practices (let alone the entire cultures they are often supposed to represent), and their development over time. We might already want to consider the taco a hybrid form not solely because of its reconfiguration from (probably) a Mexican miners' food through the migrant/Chicano urban American experience, but also because of the fraught European settler-indigene relationship that underlies Mexico itself.[1] Similarly, the problem with authenticity (well, one of them) is that it often presumes a single, stable point of reference for the "real" or authentic from which degrees of difference represent dilutions, perversions, corruptions, et cetera. As such, notions of authenticity often have a difficult time acknowledging, accounting for, and valorizing difference. I would argue that, while relevant, questions of tradition and authenticity are somewhat to the side of the conceptual issue presented by the pickerel taco, where the thing itself is such a mishmash of influences that it is difficult to decide to what authentic it might be supposed to appeal. What the pickerel taco suggests is more a question of identity than authenticity, of when and how a food ceases to be one thing and becomes another.

So, let's say Bannock wanted to do a taco because they're versatile, popular, and cheap, and with multiculturally inclusive Canadian Comfort Food as their mandate, tacos certainly figure into the culinary landscape (I have my own problems with the current vogue for "comfort food," as you can probably well imagine, given my generally shitty attitude and borderline fetishization of discomfort). Somewhere along the line, the iconic *taco de pescado* dovetails (I assume) with the Lancaster perch roll, a famously obscure ("Famous from Lancaster to Cornwall," it is sometimes said) southeastern Ontarian variation on the fish roll. Then, the flash of insight that the spongy, top-loading hot dog bun (a.k.a. "New England Style," familiar to lobster-roll fans and anyone who has ever eaten a *steamé* or *toasté* in Québec) recalls the pillowy whiteness of the steamed bun, and an inspired substitution is made. Further resonance (less charitably: Asian flair) is achieved by way of the caviar—i.e., tobiko—and tartar sauce.

One could argue that this is a crucial substitution, the steamed bun for the tortilla. That it is the timber by which the paradox of Theseus is broken[2]—the difference that makes the difference. If so slight differences in shape and preparation of the base starch are sufficient to differentiate the taco from the tostada or the sope, then so radical a substitution as a steamed bun should be still more de- or re-identifying. It is wholly speculation, but I do suspect that the fish roll plays a stronger role in the genesis of the pickerel taco than does the actual taco itself, which seems more a symbolic gloss. The choice of fish is suggestive, pickerel (a.k.a. walleye) and perch both being common fish-roll fillings and Lake Erie staples, along with the tartar, which, upon tasting, confirmed my suspicions. It is evocative of the puzzling sweetness of the topping that one receives when one is fool enough to order the fish roll "with sauce." Now, I believe enough in local authenticities ("this is how we do it here, so this is how it is done") to feel morally or at least aesthetically beholden to not decline pretty much any secret or special sauce that is proffered me—especially when done so by a sixty-year-old woman out of the window of a converted school bus, a barely anthropomorphized fish chef fryin' up his own whilst whistling a jaunty tune painted on the side—but fish-roll sauce is fucking gross. It sits somewhere between donair sauce and custard. Essential, perhaps, but perverse in that it threatens to totally eclipse the delicate flavours of the fish itself, but who am I to argue with the Woman in the Bus? In any event, it is by these associations that steamed bao for the hot dog bun substitution makes sense to me, though there is an associative link that is frustratingly, distressingly absent when one then tries to call the thing a taco. It is as if, assuming my imaginary reconstruction of the pickerel taco's origin is not far off the mark, the taco may have provided the original inspiration, but was then replaced piece by piece until it returned an utterly different ship. If this is the case, Bannock may perhaps be forgiven for wanting to hang on to the taco's currency. For although Ontarian, the perch roll is hyper local, perhaps to the point of unrecognizability, which doesn't make for the best marketing. And so the perch roll is consigned to the shadows, only to find that every element is similarly in the wings, the taco ostensibly accorded centre stage, but strangely absent in this triple substitution, where only its whispered name remains to haunt and unsettle what might otherwise be a more harmonious mingling of references.

Pulling focus somewhat, perhaps the pickerel taco suggests something greater that may be said about Canadian multiculturalism. Bannock, after all, proclaims itself a Canadian Comfort Food restaurant, describing itself thus: "Taking an honest approach to food, our dishes are dynamic and playful; they feature familiar, wholesome ingredients; and, most of all, they reflect of our country's rich regional and cultural diversity." Issues of cultural appropriation (even of reparations) are of course raised by charging fourteen dollars for two tacos (or two steamed buns, either way) at a restaurant called "Bannock" cheffed by a young white guy,[3] but the "playful dynamism" is here ramped up to such Fieriesque proportions that the place could almost be exculpated for its sheer chaotic nonsensicality (other dishes included "pad thai with tomato jam and fried beans" and "pulled pork tourtière," although it should be noted that in the interim, the menu has scaled back its Magnetic Poetry quality). I could go full Žižek and claim that, in fact, the pickerel taco is the most honest expression of Canadian multiculturalism, resting as it does upon the misrecognition of its Chinese populations as Mexican, a people less intimately bound up in the history of nation-building exploitation; which obviously perplexing gesture performs the sleight-of-hand that obscures what is happening behind the magician's back: namely, the erasure of the First Nations people for whom the restaurant's namesake stands as a symbol both of cultural identity and the normalization of settler colonialism. But then, you probably saw that coming a mile away. Returning to the Ship of Theseus analogy, perhaps there is a similarly conservative conceptual disgust at work in the (mostly, but not exclusively, anti-Islamic) xenophobia expressed by Bill C-24, the Strengthening Canadian Citizenship Act, and in Quebec's 2007–2008 Reasonable Accommodation hearings—the fear that, counter to (or as the perverse consequence of) its multicultural ideals, Canada is in danger of becoming a different ship. Does multiculturalism lead to pad thai with tomato jam and fried beans? To so-called comfort food that is so fundamentally jarring as to be unrecognizable? Is multiculturalism, in other words, stupid? I'm going to say that the answer is probably no, or at least that trendy metropolitan Canadian eatery food provides, at best, an imperfect analogy. My bad.

Really, whether the pickerel taco is not-a-taco or not-a-fish-roll is not primarily a matter of authenticity or conceptual purity. For, good lefty that I am, I find far less discomfiting something like the "Indian taco" (bannock, ground beef, lettuce, tomato, and cheese, which evokes Tex-Mex more readily than what authenticity-hounds have come to think of as a proper Mexican taco) that has become its own kind of Native comfort food, or tacos al pastor, which are fundamentally taco-shawarma hybrids born of turn-of-the-century Lebanese migration to Mexico. The real question around which I have been somewhat cowardly dancing is not simply "When does a food cease to be one thing and become another?" but, "According to whom?"

---

1 See: Jeffrey Pilcher, *Que Vivan Los Tamales!: Food and the Making of Mexican Identity* (Univeristy of New Mexico Press, 1998) and *Planet Taco: A Global History of Mexican Food* (Oxford, 2012), and Gustavo Arellano, *Taco USA: How Mexican Food Conquered America* (Scribner, 2012), for more and less academic discussions of the topic.

2 The Ship of Theseus, described by Plutarch, poses the problem of identity by asking, if a ship is mended over time until every original timber has been replaced, does it remain the same ship? My editor John made me insert this note because he assumes none of my readers have ever taken an intro philosophy course, about which, for their sakes, I hope he's right, I suppose.

3 Bannock is a kind of quick bread central to First Nations culinary culture that is also associated with poor, rural, non-aboriginal communities. The name bannock/bannach is itself apparently Scottish (from Gaelic), and the dish is generally understood to have been introduced by Scottish fur traders, although some First Nations scholars, artists, and chefs have problematized bannock's status as a colonial import. See Lisa Myers, "Best Before: Recipes and Food in Contemporary Aboriginal Art" (master's thesis, OCAD University, 2014); Peter Morin, *Bannockology: A Community Collaboration of Stories, Art, Essays, Recipes and Poems Initiated by Liard Valley Literary Society* (Open Space Arts Society, 2009); and Martin Reinhardt's Decolonizing Diet project.

Postscript: On Italicization

This seems as good a place as any to comment on some of the conceptual issues posed by loan-word italicization. In practical terms, the matter is quite simple, and one of house style. The publisher adopts a particular dictionary as a standard, and italicizes accordingly: if a given "foreign" word is italicized in the dictionary, it is italicized in the text. This is, however, a deferral of engagement, rather than a response to the question of what gets italicized and why. We might ask how the dictionary of choice decides what words are italicized, and whether this rationale is transparently stated and available to the user. The answer to this question is, as far as I can tell, rarely. Even the gargantuan *Compact Oxford English Dictionary* (1971) that I use for most things (quite inconveniently, since Invisible's dictionary of choice is the *Canadian Oxford Dictionary*, which differs in some things), with its thirty-two pages of Historical Introduction and General Explanation, does not (as far as I can tell) explicitly state the authors' philosophy of italicization for foreign words, although it does offer this eloquent comment on its philosophy of vocabulary:

> The Vocabulary of a widely-diffused and highly-cultivated living language is not a fixed quantity circumscribed by definite limits. That vast aggregate of words and phrases which constitutes the Vocabulary of English-speaking men [sic] presents, to the mind that endeavours to grasp it as a definite whole, the aspect of one of those nebulous masses familiar to the astronomer, in which a clear and unmistakable nucleus shades off on all sides through zones of decreasing

brightness, to a dim marginal film that seems to end nowhere, but to lose itself imperceptibly in the surrounding darkness.

Avoiding for the moment the implication that other languages reside in a sort of cosmic darkness, if we follow this metaphor, we may view the practice of italicization as the negotiation of such a "shading off," describing the limits of resolution for our view of the nebulous mass called English. This negotiation is performed differently by different sources at different times. Absent a superior authority, the rule followed by the dictionary's authors cannot but be one of currency—the more widespread a word becomes in English, the less call there is for its italicization—tempered by a spirit of either conservatism or inclusiveness. It is probable that some dictionaries take a bibliometric approach to measuring currency, but this still entails an arbitrary judgment of how current is current enough. For example, the *Canadian Oxford Dictionary* does not italicize taco, or banh mi, or kimchi. Indeed, to have italicized *taco* everywhere in this book would have been not only visually jarring, but bordering on the pretentious, by rendering conspicuous a word that for all intents and purposes has become English. Which is to say that it sits easily in and falls effortlessly from English-speaking mouths, in a way that *taco de pescado* may not. So loose a rule as nimble the tongue, though! It seems absurd to italicize spaghetti, but less so *casarecce* or *maltagliati*. Quebec presents its own peculiarities, with its fraught history of linguistic nationalism. Depanneur and poutine are presented here and in the *Canadian Oxford* without italics, but one could imagine some resenting the English assimilation of these words, as they resent the "intrusion" of English words into Quebec speech. The Office québécois de la langue française embodies the notion that the State has a role in policing language, although the degree of linguistic interpenetration in practice suggests a more permissive attitude on the part of many Québécois/es. The *steamé* and *toasté* referred to earlier, denoting hot dogs served in a steamed bun or toasted bun, respectively (typically with yellow mustard, chopped onion, and cabbage), are good examples of the hybridity of Québécois French.

But let's take a step back. I suggest above that *taco* is a word that for all intents and purposes has become English. This may be true in the most casual sense of "for all intents and purposes," but the casual approach may not be the most attuned one. What does it mean for a word to "become English," or be barred from such becoming? Authors such as Junot Díaz, Gloria Anzaldúa, and Lourdes Torres have argued for the significance of code-switching (alternating between languages) and the refusal to italicize or translate Spanish words and passages as a way of destabilizing the hegemony of English in American letters. Díaz, who has received the most public attention for this position (as a Pulitzer-winning novelist, whereas Anzaldúa's and Torres's works are comparatively unknown outside of academic circles), has put it thus:

For me allowing the Spanish to exist in my text without the benefit of italics or quotations marks a very important political move. Spanish is not a minority language. Not in this hemisphere, not in the United States, not in the world inside my head. So why treat it like one? Why "other" it? Why de-normalize it? By keeping Spanish as normative in a predominantly English text, I wanted to remind readers of the mutability of languages. And to mark how steadily English is transforming Spanish and Spanish is transforming English.[1]

A somewhat different set of considerations may apply in the case of monolingual anglophone writers (i.e., my case[2]), however. Here the political valence of the de-italicizing gesture is more problematic, the difference hinted at by the fact that "de-italicization" might more accurately be referred to as "romanizing." An argument can be made that the integration or assimilation into English of words from other languages bears an element of appropriation, particularly in light of claims that such anglicization often involves obscuring a word's history and provenance, or its specificity in the "donor" language. Something is always lost when a word is removed from its relational context and repositioned in a new one (something is also added, of course, but we cannot assume that this transformation is necessarily power-neutral). In this respect, the decision to italicize a word that is not italicized in the dictionary of choice may also be seen as a way of destabilizing linguistic normativity, in that it renders problematic the assimilation of the word by retaining its Otherness. The italics may insist on the word's relationality within a system of meaning and practices that is not the linguistic context in which it currently appears. Of course, we can't assume the success of such a textual strategy, for it is also a common occurrence for Anglo writers to pepper their texts with italicized foreign words to mobilize their perceived exoticism/authenticity as a source of cultural capital. I was hoping to cap this off with a glib Latin quotation to the effect that there are no sure things in radical criticism, but owing to the bias toward general principles and universal rules that is quite literally the definition of a maxim, I had no such luck.

Suffice to say, for the most part we have adhered to the dictionary-of-choice rule in this text, and any exceptions to this rule are conscious, considered, and intentional. They should be seen as invitations to reflect on the particular significance of the word or phrase as presented, its history and its multiple meanings, what is gained and what is lost by rendering it conspicuous or inconspicuous on the page. Further, they are invitations to reflect on the role not only of language, but of literal text and the conventions thereof as forms of embodied criticism or thought that do more than communicate information; to consider the rhetorical infrastructure of text. Also, some of them may be typos.

---

1 Quoted in Evelyn Nien-Ming Ch'ien, *Weird English* (Harvard University Press, 2004), 204. See also Lourdes Torres, "In the Contact Zone: Code-Switching Strategies by Latino/a Writers," *MELUS* vol. 32, no. 1., 2007; Gloria Anzaldúa, *Borderlands/La Frontera: The New Mestiza* (Aunt Lute Books, 1987), and *The Gloria Anzaldúa Reader*, edited by AnaLouise Keating (Duke University Press, 2007). The latter articulates Anzaldúa's position on italicization, whereas the 1987 edition of *Borderlands/La Frontera* does italicize its Spanish passages, interestingly enough. For an introduction to these issues from the perspective of editorial policy, see Katey Trnka, "Foreign Word Alert, Foreign Word Alert: Rethinking Editorial Approaches to the Italicization of Foreign Terms," Portland State University PDXScholar.

2 While I consider myself bilingual, my spoken French is far from fluent, and my written, execrable.

Don't Take Your Sword to the Table?

For the politics and politesse of dietary constraints and the guest/host relationship, *debate* is probably too strong a word, but it is certainly a fraught issue on both sides of which I have found myself at different times in my life. I have spoken to many people—lapsed, lapsing, and pro-lapsed vegans and vegetarians—who explained that they did not want, for their hosts' sakes, to find themselves in situations where they could not eat what was put before them. This is laudable as a matter of courtesy, but also as a recognition of the essential role of food as a social coher-ent,[1] and of the importance for many people of being able to provide for the nourishment, and share in the nourish-ment, of another. Breaking bread together, and all that.

This is not a one-way street. The egalitarianism implied by sharing food—the recognition that, fundamentally, we are all united by our mortality, our need to pause, to rest, to eat—suggests a willingness to meet one's guest halfway, as it were. Food is the bridge, and it is upon that bridge we meet, held aloft however precariously over the chasm of difference. I refrain from using the language of duty or obli-gation on either party's part, because that is not what I'm trying to get at. It is, in fact, exactly what I am trying to get away from. When hosting, one wants to have one's guest feel comfortable, safe, and (potentially) at home. This need not follow from an ethical imperative, but arises out of co-feeling, of compassion. Thus, to place before someone a food with which they are uncomfortable, or which they cannot eat, for political or constitutional reasons, is to inter-rupt that circuit of compassion and mutuality. To aver in an authoritative tone that one should "eat what is put before them" is to succumb to the stridency of the wounded ego, and become again the Master of the House, at whose board the *philia* of the neighbour is at pains to survive.

I recently heard a pastry chef from a famed NYC avant-garde restaurant reflect on the tensions between virtuoso celebrity restaurateuring and what somebody (not me) might call an "ethics of care" in cooking:

> If a friend of mine was coming over for Thanksgiving and brought a guest I didn't know, and that guest ended up being a vegan or disliking turkey or having an issue, as much as that's inconvenient to me, or goes against what I had planned, you're in my home and you're uncomfortable, and I'm going to figure out a way to make you happy. You know, I feel like that has to kind of be the starting point. Otherwise, a lot of people lose why they started cooking in the first place... I made Jell-O for my mom when I was six and it made her cry; that was the starting point. It's funny how far you can go and how that can get lost, and I think it's important not to lose it.[2]

Pride, then, is something that should be left at the threshold even in one's own home, to emerge again in concert at the table, from the satisfaction of the host to have provided for the happiness and satiety of one, and of the honour of the guest to have dined at the table of the other. What pride we arrive at should thus be born of the recognition of the pleasure of good company, of being together.

That said, are we expected to honour the whims, the fickle prejudices, whatever provincialisms our guests carry with them? Of course not. Or, you know, maybe? Just as a guest—vegan, celiac, mycophobe—must respect what is at stake in their refusal to eat, so too must those who take wild offence at what they see as a vegan's fundamental ingratitude re-examine what they are presupposing the table represents. The claim that such ethical conceits as vegetarianism or veganism should acquiesce to the social function and decorum of the table is not far from the insistence upon unity and uniformity that is so essential and yet so dangerous in the formation and performance of the nation or, equally, of the nationalist struggle. It is indeed the crisis of the Other that lends such tension to the act of eating together, itself a performance, presumption, and production of commonality. The question of how much Otherness can be accommodated before the circuit of compassion breaks down is problematic as much for the meal as for the nation, the movement, the community. It is this sharing that is supposed to both transcend and align each of us in our indissoluble difference, and is simultaneously jeopardized by that same difference.

This is a conceptual analogy, and I do not want to stray too far from dinner itself, for it is precisely the difference between dinner and nation that I am trying to elucidate here, even if one remains a flashpoint for the other, as controversies over halal school lunch options in France, England, Canada, and the United States have recently demonstrated. Importantly, what the nation cannot rely on— affect, compassion, and good humour—is precisely in what spirit dinner must be assembled.[3] It is a mistake to couch the work of the host and the guest in the language of duty and obligation, as is often done. Rather, it is essential that such work remain beyond or before the Law, which is not to say pre- or a-political, but on a terrain where the political, as a negotiation of love and trust and the basic necessities of living together, remains in process. If we seek to codify such

interaction, we risk falling back into the labyrinth of man-
ners and affectations that suborn the vital political into vacu-
ous politicking. So I guess what I'm saying is Hannah Arendt
can take her *polis* as space of freedom only for those freed
of need or the thought of need and, you know, mourn it.[4]

---

1 I am fully aware that *coherent* is not a noun, but can't it be? A "coher-
ent" as that which imparts/participates in coherence? That which, as a
depressant depresses, and an adulterant adulterates, coheres? I think it is
a successful nominalization.

2 WD-50's Alex Stupak in conversation with Adam Gopnik for the *New
Yorker* podcast. Another point of interest from the interview is when
Stupak makes his appeal for the term "technoemotional cooking," in lieu
of "molecular gastronomy" or "modernist cuisine." Although still just
as unpleasant to say or read, technoemotional cooking—along similar
lines to the previous discussion of Pomiane and technical precision as a
dimension of love—at least attempts to counter the impressions of cold-
ness, calculation, and heartless abstraction that may be evoked by the
terms. Much of the anxiety and incredulity of the pedestrian response
to molecular gastronomy seem to hinge on the denaturing of the food,
but I have found a lot of the big "molecular" cooks tend to talk a lot
about using high technique as a way of getting playful with the emotional
associations we have with food (Adrià in *El Bulli: Cooking in Process*, for
example), even evincing a sort of nostalgic romanticism very much in
line with the *friands* of Pomiane's childhood.

3 Hence the notion of law justified by making up for the moral deficit of
its subjects, if you buy that kind of thing.

4 This may seem an oblique reference, coming seemingly out of
nowhere. Even I, upon rereading this in manuscript form, had to pause
and ask, "What did I mean by that?" So, doing you and me both a
favour, what I am referring to here is Arendt's desire, expressed in *The*

Human Condition (University of Chicago Press, 1958), to recuperate a model of Athenian democracy as part of her critique of modern political life. Accordingly freedom, or philosophy, or truly political thought and action, can only exist in the space of *polis* or public space. The *polis* is defined in opposition to the *oikos* – the private sphere, the space of the home, of animal necessity and the provision for those needs, indeed the space of social reproduction. Freedom must be freedom from need. Now, obviously Arendt's analysis goes well beyond some reaffirmation of the separation of public/private in the modern sense, but I still think this is a problematic place to start, and that perhaps there is a conception of politics and even of freedom that proceeds from or within the realm of need and nourishment, rather than being predicated only upon its satisfaction. So that's what I meant. Leave no quip unfootnoted!

Fish Stew and Duelling Authenticities

I have for some years been attempting to forge a New Year's Eve tradition of making a big pot of bouillabaisse and refusing to go out anywhere. As you are in all likelihood well aware, there is perhaps no surer way to begin your year with a fresh measure of dyspepsia and regret than to heed your friends' naive eleventh-hour petitions to go out to this or that party that supposedly will be "fun," and I like to think that a giant fish stew and a surfeit of wine should provide adequate protection against such poor decision-making (lamentably, I have yet to be vindicated in this).

In inviting someone over for bouillabaisse, however, I sometimes take pause and ask myself, "Is this really bouillabaisse I have to offer?" I would hate to have someone over under false pretenses, and the invocation of this very festive-sounding French classic certainly excites more, uh, excitement than the pedestrian "Hey, want to come over for some miscellaneous fish stew?" But miscellaneous is, in a truer (well, let's say true-ish) sense, exactly what bouillabaisse is, isn't it? Bouillabaisse is to Marseille what the po' boy is to New Orleans, in many ways: an intensely local, identifiable, signature dish that resolutely refuses to be pinned down as to of what exactly it is comprised. A sort of culinary shibboleth, but one that does not admit any single authoritative form, while still providing ample opportunities to decry the inauthentic as it moves beyond its locality (or, arguably, as its localities multiply). *Larousse Gastronomique* reads, "There are as many 'authentic' bouillabaisses as there are ways of combining fish," a strangely even-handed assertion for a culture far better known for its prescriptive than descriptive temperament in matters gastronomical. But it gets at what is most interesting about bouillabaisse. Like many now-refined and canonized dishes, bouillabaisse began as poor people's food, a fisherman's stew made up from the many bony and bellicose-looking sea creatures that were deemed not fit for market. The name itself derives from the French verbs *bouillir* (to boil) and *abaisser* (to reduce), which one must do a lot of when dealing with a motley assortment of animals that all demand their own cooking times. Bouillabaisse, it could thus be said, is more a method of preparation than a recipe per se.

Even the 1980 Marseille *Charte de la Bouillabaisse* stops short of imposing a strict definition, although it recommends minimum requirements for the inclusion of certain types of fish. *Rascasse*, one of the fish long held to be essential to bouillabaisse, is usually translated into English as "scorpionfish," although in French *rascasse* refers to a more taxonomically irreverent collection of species ranging across several genera, and even whole orders. Hence, in spite of the translation, the fish in the category "scorpionfish" may not perfectly align with those considered *rascasse* and thus essential to the identity of the soup. But maybe less important than what *rascasse* really is, is the historical fact that local nomenclature does not always transpose neatly across languages and locales, and often still less across folk and scientific (ichthyological) classificatory systems. Granted, even the most devoted stickler is unlikely to cry bullshit so long as the fish is spiny and poisonous-looking enough, but this taxonomic ambiguity highlights the peculiarity of what is the "difference that makes a difference" and how destabilizing it can be for notions of authenticity.

Or maybe it doesn't? A. J. Liebling, in his 1962 *New Yorker* essay "The Soul of Bouillabaisse Town," wades deep into this taxonomic quagmire and arrives eventually at the conclusion that: "This is a world of constantly diminishing certainties, and the disappearance of even a negative one is a heavy loss; never again would I be able to say with assurance that there was no *rascasse* in America." Perhaps in the 1960s this disappearance of certainties felt more urgent and destabilizing than in our own historical moment, when permeability of boundaries is the order of the day. And perhaps the *rascasse* turns out to be one of those culinary shibboleths, the insistence thereupon but a synecdoche for the assertion that bouillabaisse simply cannot be made "true" outside of Marseille? But true to whom? Is the authentic bouillabaisse that which contains more of the "right" fish or that which contains what is cheapest and freshest at a given moment? To which spirit are we enjoined to be true: that of the restaurateur protecting the integrity of the local specialty or that of the (perhaps mythical) fisherman? For my own part, I'm going to go say the fisherman, and you can mistake that for romanticism if you want, but I actually just want to be able to spend more money on booze.

With Friends Like These...

For someone who professes not to be a great fan of sweets, I certainly devote a lot of thought to chocolate bars. Possibly it has to do with the act of procuring a chocolate bar, which provides the sort of minor interruption of routine that is so conducive to private reflection. If it happens that I have spent the majority of a day in my house (and it bodes that I may spend the remaining hours there as well), I am more likely to step out for the sole purpose of acquiring a chocolate bar than any other solitary item. It really does feel like giving oneself a break. The task has the pleasing brevity and single-mindedness such that it does not make one feel that one has committed to an errand, but does satisfy the urge to see the sky and feel the air on one's skin, without the bother and pageantry of sitting about in the grass, becoming damp and scratchy, as is so often the case. (Why is it so difficult to read in the park? Must one always have a blanket? Annoying.) To the dep and back is not much time for serious reflection, but I often feel in those passages a calm and clarity that usually attends the contemplation of a serene nature, or at least less-cluttered vistas than that of the dilapidated, elevated highway that serves as the northern horizon of my neighbourhood.

I should mention that the chocolate bar, as the object of such outings, has a bit of its own aura, for in my years of veganism, the casual chocolate bar was effectively removed from my terrain of possibilities. It was with something of a shock of familiarity that I first realized, in some early summer of my post-veganism, that I was completely free to take a walk down the street and just buy a chocolate bar, at any old store, pretty much whenever I wanted. I don't know that it is easy to convey the specialness of this, but it is something that retains even now the slight thrill of novelty. There is something to it of an entry back into the normal, the capacity to participate in the mundane and common-place of society, like cutting one's hair or voting or staying in a hotel, that punks and other sundry weirdos go through much of their life excluded and excluding themselves from. It always feels like an achievement, like one has just barely pulled one over on the world.

Today, on such an amble, I got to wondering about how effectively chocolate bars could serve as links to the past. Certainly, all foods carry some potential for time travel, which has been roundly exploited in literature both high and low, but the heavily processed quality of choco-late bars (and other candies, of course) allows for the greater likelihood that the constitution and preparation of a chocolate bar remains unchanged for five, ten, even twenty years. Admittedly, what with fluctuating prices of cocoa, corn, cane, and nougat, changing dietary trends, and an industry fixation on novelty, such consistency is by no means guaranteed. But the possibility suggests itself. This was, in fact, about as far as I got in my ruminations over the block and a half between the dep and my house, spurred by my puzzlement as to whether the Twix I was eating, once my favourite chocolate bar (I don't recall over how many years, but it's one of those shelved-away biographical factoids that when I was a little kid, Twix was my favourite, as Orange Crush was my favourite pop), was slightly stale or whether some change in the consis-tency of caramel had been engineered. I thought I had a good sensual profile of what a Twix tasted like, and that it had roughly "always" tasted so, and what I was currently eating deviated somehow.

Through some associative quantum stumble (something less than a "Quantum Leap", for you eighties TV babies), the next thing to spring to mind was some feeling of ancient mortification associated with the Pal-o-Mine, a bar the particulars of which to this day I cannot recall. Save that, like a Twix, it consists of two pieces—a bar always already twain. The stark outlines of a memory related to a Pal-o-Mine stand out in my psyche, but with an equally striking absence of detail. The outlines of what? Some unpleasantness. An embarrassment? A disappointment? A foundational youthful disillusionment? I don't know, it's all too Freudian. I only recall that it took place at a historical tourism village to which my class was taken on a field trip; I imagine I was between the ages of six and nine, and there was a Pal-o-Mine involved.

I know that the chocolate bar was my only purchase of the day—perhaps I had never tasted one and was woefully dissatisfied? Maybe some literal interpretation of the name of the bar, too late apprehended, left me beholden to share half of it with another child, surely a minor tragedy for such a penny-pinching young glutton as I remember myself to have been? Or, still more tragicomic, did I feel that flush of humiliation rise to upon realizing that I had purchased a chocolate bar designed to be shared with one's bosom friend, highlighting the sad fact that I had no such bud? Is it thus the silent mockery of the second portion that impressed itself upon me, to be felt however hazily so many years later?

Possibly it was the frustration and embarrassment of buying a Pal-o-Mine on the mistaken assumption that it was an old-timey chocolate bar, seeing as I was buying it from a period drugstore—you know, like the kind of chocolate bar the pioneers ate—only to have it pointed out by a mercilessly perceptive pretween lout that it was the kind of bar that could be had at any corner store, and further, that it was of an inferior and "gaywad" persuasion. Yet another squandered opportunity to affirm through an act of petty consumerism my normality, in the vain hope of diverting attention from my precocious vocabulary and hand-me-down Esprit T-shirt (that I had so proudly strutted about in until being informed that Esprit was clothing for girls) that indelibly marked me as socially just that side of the pale.

Perhaps, in order to fill out the details, it remains for me to simply eat piles of the chocolate bar until I have my epiphany. But this assumes that recall will come with repeated exposure, and that the recipe of the Pal-o-Mine has not mutated over the intervening decades, compromising the exactitude of the sense-memory relationship. Perhaps the rest of the picture will never be found in the bar, which can at best continue to repeat indefinitely and with gradual loss of strength the same garbled testimony. Only the surround remains—low scrub, weathered wood, and eighteenth-century pioneer reenactment, all shot through with the vivid and abiding shame at which the young are such adepts.

Thank Heaven for Small Failures

Somewhere along the line, the Oh Henry! became my favourite chocolate bar. I cannot account for how this happened. It was certainly not one of my favourites growing up, the "fudge" inside so unlike the dense brown-sugar fudges of my mother, the gummy chocolate varieties of my friends' parents,[1] or the creamy yet resilient fudge one bought from old women at the flea market along with those lollipops that were just a lobster-shaped piece of chocolate on a stick (a regionalism, surely). There was something so very dull-seeming about the Oh Henry!, like a lumpy, unfinished, poor man's Turtle (or would that be the GooGoo Cluster?). I must have been more of a wafer man, because I remember Kit Kat and Coffee Crisp jockeying for the favoured position much of my young life.

Now, in the twilight of my youth (or, arguably, the loathsome murky dawn of my middle age, depending on how long I expect to keep this up), it is certainly a sign of something that this workhorse of a bar, the homely yet reliable Oh Henry!, has come to occupy the seat of my affection, and no less its permutations: the Peanut Butter Oh Henry!, the Honey Roasted Peanut Oh Henry!, and the seasonal Oh Henry! Egg. The Egg is not, as you might expect, an "egg" along the lines of the Cadbury Creme Egg, but just a roughly ovular mass of Oh Henry!. The resemblance is faint, but I suppose there is no holiday appropriate to the marketing of an Oh Henry! Lump of Turd (Valentine's Day, maybe?), so Easter, and thus egg, it had to be. Luckily, like many seasonal confections and failed spinoffs, they are available year-round at your local Dollarama.

I first started enjoying, or at least first started buying, Oh Henry! bars when the corner store down the block from my parents' house started selling the Peanut Butter Oh Henry! bars two-for-a-dollar. At that point, so keen on maximizing the money-to-candy ratio of my meagre allowance, I would have bought any two things for a dollar. But it was the PBOH, and consequently I developed a taste for them. This was the old Peanut Butter Oh Henry!, of course, circa probably '93, long before the advent of the Reese Peanut Butter Oh Henry!, which I like less than the original. It's minor, but what really gets me is that there is a very thin, but still perceptible, crisp layer of some sort, like the ossified membrane of a prehistoric fish (Probably not like that at all. Do membranes even ossify? Membranes don't ossify, right?) around the peanut-butter inside that still throws me off. I've written before on the strangeness of a chocolate bar so long taken for granted being made eerily unfamiliar.[2] The case of the PBOH's Reesification is not quite the same, because I can pinpoint the difference, but sometimes those little differences can feel like some *Invasion of the Body Snatchers*/Capgras syndrome shit. The point is, I figure it was this cheap availability of PBOH that got me into the Oh Henry! in the first place. It does not fully explain my drift into fondness for the original Oh Henry!, but it at least brings us one step closer to solving this awesome mystery.

The Honey Roasted Peanut Oh Henry! (hereafter HRPOH) seemed like a bit of a gamble initially, and when I first tried it, I wasn't totally convinced. The differences between it and a regular Oh Henry! are, admittedly, slight. The honey is almost undetectable, but I am willing to believe that the bar is sweeter, and the peanuts are slightly crisper, more delicate, as one would expect of honey-roasted peanuts. Only by this juxtaposition can you consciously appreciate that in a normal Oh Henry! the peanuts are, as it were, raw—almost vegetal—in comparison. It is a good bar. Though I have made an about-face in my opinion of the HRPOH, and sometimes crave it specifically in lieu of a regular Oh Henry!, I think it has also made me appreciate the original all the more; I've become more cognizant of its particular charms. There is something endearing about the oafishness of the original that is lacking in the inexplicably more refined HRPOH. It really depends on what kind of company one is in the mood for.

Anyway, the other day I was passing through downtown, grumbling, no doubt, about the lack of snow, and was seized by the desire for a chocolate bar. Speculating that it might brighten my mood somewhat, I stepped into one of those sad downtown depanneurs (I don't know why I feel this way about deps in downtown Montreal. Perhaps I pity them for having to rely entirely on the patronage of people who live in downtown Montreal, at the same time that I resent as slightly evil their quite understandably obscene beer prices) and was surprised to find one Honey Roasted Peanut Oh Henry! sitting amongst the regular Oh Henry! bars. So, praising my good fortune (because I hadn't had one in a while), I purchased it. Now, there are two things that make this story worth recounting:

1. There was a small note taped to the counter that read, "IS THIS THE END OF CAPITALISM?"

2. The chocolate bar was extremely stale. Not inedibly so, because I certainly ate it, but undeniably so.

There was something about these things taken together that brightened my mood so much more than I could have anticipated. There is the perverse satisfaction I sometimes derive from things going wrong, i.e., putting stock arbitrarily in a thing only to have it up and spit remorselessly in one's face. Or perhaps it was because I do find something comforting in the *tendre indifférence du monde*, as it were, the idea of a universe in which "everything happens for a reason" being much more deeply terrifying and disheartening to me. The former leaves us freer to enjoy the delicate humour in life's little failures, a humour that I find touches me almost like music, in that I can detect its touch, but can neither explain nor understand it. And here, by way of the cryptic note taped to the counter, there is the added mysterious consonance of so unexpected a sentiment of economic pessimism (or political optimism?), along with the experience of paying $1.69 for a stale, piece-of-shit chocolate bar. It's basically Liszt, people.[3]

---

1 Which fudge somehow in the symbolic register of my family's relationship to the outside world came to be thought of as the fudge equivalent of white bread—undeniably vulgar, yet exotic and desirable. As if one could with any credibility decry the nutritional content of one fudge compared to another—can the addition of marshmallows really cheapen something that is already entirely made out of sugar? Apparently, the answer was yes.

2 See "With Friends Like These..."

3 Or perhaps Ryuichi Sakamoto. I'm thinking someone with a lighter touch.

Postscript: On Fudge

Since writing in passing about fudge in connection with Oh Henry! bars, I have been reminded that this is the second time in so many days that the uncertain identity of fudge has come up. Looking at a package of Fudge Covered Ritz that a friend brought back from America, I wondered aloud what it was that made them fudge-covered as opposed to chocolate-covered. She speculated that it was because they weren't made with real chocolate, and I could well imagine that the big wheels down at the Ritz factory would have no truck with such obviously second-rate language as "chocolatey." Fudge, in this case, seems an inspired evasion.

But thinking about Oh Henry! bars, and how alien the "fudge" therein has always seemed to my image of fudge, got me wondering what's up with fudge, anyway? What makes fudge fudge, and where does it come from? I ended up hauling out both volumes of my monstrous *Oxford English Dictionary*, because curiously *fudge* in its present usage only makes it into the supplement of the 1971 edition, appearing on page 3,972 of the second volume, as the fifth sense of the word: "A soft-grained sweetmeat prepared by boiling together milk, sugar, butter, and chocolate or maple sugar." Of US origin, 1897 (why it took more than a half-century for this sense of the word to make it into the dictionary is anyone's guess).

The rest of the not-inconsiderable space devoted to *fudge* has to do with the term as something shouted to express incredulity or disfavour: "Contemptible nonsense, 'stuff,' bosh," or the not altogether different:

To fit together in a clumsy, makeshift, or dishonest manner... To make (a problem) look as if it had been correctly worked, by altering figures; to conceal the defects of (a map or other drawing) by adjustment of the parts, so that no glaring disproportion is observed; and in other like uses. (vol. 1, p.1090)

Both of the latter meanings I had assumed followed upon the confectionary sense, although it appears that these others enjoy priority by a good two hundred or so years. Both senses are of obscure and potentially unrelated origin, although possible candidates include the namesake of some lying pig of a seventeenth-century English sea captain, and still curiouser, "An onomatopoeic alteration of FADGE (v.), with the vowel expressive of more clumsy action." Not to interrupt your head-scratching, because it took me a minute to figure this one out, too, but *fadge* is an obsolete term meaning to fit well, or make fit well, get along, or fit well into place. *Fudge*, then, is almost its opposite, a clumsy dissembling of *fadge*: hence *fudge* is a fudging of the word *fadge*. I know, right?

On top of this, a few hundred years later, you have American boarding-school debs applying the term to a delicious sugary confection that gradually makes its way into the lexicon, as I understand it, as a thing-in-itself. Perhaps I'm just out of the loop on this, but do people in general think of fudge the food as some kind of chump job trying to pull a fast one? If so, what is it trying to pass itself off as? It's a brown square.

On Nigella Lawson, Impossible Witnessing, and the Reification of Analysis

I have long had a lazy appreciation for Nigella Lawson. It has its roots in the one time I stumbled upon her show whilst channel-surfing in some location where there were channels to surf; I assume either a hotel room or my parents' house. I was surprised by how engaging and articulate she was (had I been aware at the time of her prior history as a book and restaurant columnist who read Medieval and Modern Languages at Oxford, I would have been less surprised), and the casual way that the camera moved around the space of her very real-seeming (possibly really real?) kitchen. I have it in my head that the segment was predicated on her coming home after a night of drinking, and eating an entire pan of sticky toffee pudding she whips up on the fly, but that is probably a figment.

If her warmth, eloquence, and wit are not absent from the popular discourse around Lawson, they are certainly eclipsed by commentary on her beauty, her sexuality, and the perceived flirtatiousness of her aesthetic. Lawson herself has taken issue with the sexualization of her image. Even or especially where is concerned her notorious "salted caramel facial" photo shoot for the 2010 issue of *Stylist* magazine she guest-edited, Lawson remains insistent that she has no interest in being, as she has in the past been dubbed, the "queen of food porn." The cover frames her face in close-up, eyes closed, lips parted slightly in a smile; there is an abundance of glistening caramel. It does not necessarily strike one as unsexual.

I know it is said but my honest opinion is that I have quite an intense and honest rapport with the camera. I don't think I'm flirtatious. That makes me cringe. However, I can see that I am not a skinny woman and the male gaze is such that whatever is there is seen to be there for their benefit."[1]

What I find (intellectually) provocative about this statement is her dual insistence that sensualized and sexualized are not mutually reducible phenomena, and that male spectatorship is not the *ne plus ultra* of representation. While Lawson's use of the phrase "the male gaze" here seems more generalized than Laura Mulvey's original formulation of the term in her 1975 essay "Visual Pleasure and Narrative Cinema," I have no reason to believe that Lawson would not be familiar with the concept. The male gaze for Mulvey described the formal and narrative conventions (in Hollywood film specifically, although the concept has been widely influential and now generalized to literary, as well as visual, strategies of representation) through which women are produced as implicitly sexually receptive, mere objects for men's scopophilic pleasure. The concept has been heavily revised over time, but central to it is that under patriarchy, visual representation is ordered by the logic of a male looker, indeed a voyeur, and a female who exists to be looked at.[2]

When Lawson states that the *Stylist* photo is about representing an unapologetic, "rapturous joy in caramel," one might roll one's eyes at what one takes an affectation of naïveté, but I think that there is an important point about female pleasure embedded there. Effectively, she is insisting on not only the possibility, but the immanence of female sensual pleasure, represented in print/on television, that is neither constituted for nor defined by a hegemonic male spectator. I do not mean to suggest Nigella as a critical feminist icon, or that it is this easy to step outside the libidinal economy of patriarchy, but I think that taking such declarations of pleasure—arguably of agency—seriously is part of the critical work of interrogating phallocentrism. To deny the relevance of the subject's own interpretation and experience is in a curious way to participate actively in their objectification, by foreclosing the possibility of a female pleasure that is not wholly defined and recuperated by the male spectator. By assuming the total hegemony of the male gaze as that which organizes all representation and all looking, we effectively render impossible the witnessing of female pleasure for itself.

I see this as representative of what we might call the reification of analysis, whereby a particular theory or analytic lens becomes so powerful as to begin to eclipse what it is meant to elucidate. Or, put another way, that it comes to be seen as so good at taking something apart in a particular way that we can no longer conceive of the thing (idea, phenomenon, et cetera) being made up of any other parts. In this case, I'm referring to a particular stream of feminist criticism, but it is commonplace across all academic disciplines, and perhaps becomes all the more common as concepts and theoretical tools move into other domains and enjoy more popular currency.

There is an analogy to be made here, if you will please forgive the incongruity of scale of importance, with the anti-sex-work rationale of some second-wave feminism that defines sex work as inherently exploitative and thus nonconsensual, since one cannot "rationally" consent to one's own exploitation. We see the institutionalization of this analysis in Bill C-36, which, in the wake of the landmark Bedford case that found Canada's prostitution laws unconstitutional, effectively continues the marginalization and stigmatization of sex workers.[3] The Protection of Communities and Exploited Persons Act presents a set of laws that intertwine the benevolent paternalism of the (patriarchal) state with the radical critique of sexual relations of second-wave feminism, appealing to both social conservatives and anti-sex-work liberal feminists. Ostensibly designed to protect exploited individuals, Bill C-36 essentially defines all sex workers as sui generis exploited. Thus, the analytically and historically useful concept of all heterosexual sex under patriarchal capitalism being a form of violence, and sex work merely the least adorned version thereof, no longer serves to denormalize asymmetrical gender relations, but instead comes to enjoy the status of evidence itself, a form of evidence that precludes actually listening to or taking seriously the accounts of many sex workers, as was demonstrated by the justice committee hearings on the bill.[4] By virtue of the theory, we may take the structure for granted, the analysis becomes the object itself, and the lived realities and analyses of those most directly concerned are occluded, incidental. (The sex workers and those who work with them become another kind of impossible witness.) This can be described as a reification of analysis to the extent that the analytic apparatus no longer helps us to engage with the world beyond its face value, but stands in, as something more real than the people, the voices, the pleasures, that are being disclosed, but which it cannot accommodate.

This may seem very far removed from the image of a British celebrity cook with a bunch of caramel on her face, but although the stakes are different, I see a formal continuity between the two. The concept of the male gaze is extremely valuable insofar as it offers a tool for thinking about the politics of representation, and to the extent that it describes how in the day-to-day male privilege conceives its right to look, to comment, to catcall, as sacrosanct (one only needs to be a woman and have walked down a street, had a job, taken a drink of water, ever done basically anything, et cetera), but it should not define the limits of analysis. I think there is something powerful in Nigella Lawson's refusal to acquiesce to the reading of her presentation as sexual, and her insistence on its sensuality, for her, and on her terms. The male gaze of course sees "salted caramel bukkake" (I apologize for even writing that, but it had a lot of currency on comment threads, *quel surprise*) and reads it as an image that exists for the titillation of the presumed male audience, but Nigella denies the male gaze the privilege of defining the meaning of the image by asserting the existence, nay the ontological primacy, of another reality, the reality of her own gastronomic pleasure.

"I wanted to make food and my slavering passion for it the starting point," Lawson writes, "indeed, for me it was the starting point. I have nothing to declare but my greed."

---

1 "Nigella Lawson on the Male Gaze, 'I Want Never Gets,' and Not Being A Chef," *Eater* (blog), November 16, 2010.

2 Laura Mulvey, "Visual Pleasure and Narrative Cinema" *Screen*, vol. 16(3), Autumn 1975.,

3 In Canada (AG) v. Bedford [2010], the Supreme Court ruled in favour of Terri-Jean Bedford, Amy Lebovitch, and Valerie Scott, who had argued that Canadian prostitution laws (against "keeping or being found in a bawdy house," "living on the avails of prostitution," and "communicating in public for the purpose of prostitution," whereas sex work itself is not illegal) violated sex workers' right to security of the person, and were therefore unconstitutional. The ruling created an opportunity for the drafting of legislation that would better protect sex worker's rights and

empower them to create safer working conditions. Bill C-36, the Protection of Communities and Exploited Persons Act, which passed in 2014, has been widely criticized by sex workers' groups such as Stella and the Canadian Alliance for Sex Work Law Reform for continuing to marginalize and stigmatize sex work.

4 http://www.pivotlegal.org/justice_committee_ignored_sex_workers

"Such Praise Inspires with Diviner Lust Your Friends, Who Guttle with Greater Gust"[1]

Someone once told me something interesting about the G sounds in linguistics, but I don't remember what it was. I am inclined to think it had something to do with the prevalence of G words involved in eating, specifically eating to excess, although they seem to derive equally, and perhaps not coincidentally (if we want to make some claims about grotesque topography in Rabelais's *Gargantua and Pantagruel*) from other words for large size, anatomy, geographical formations, and the formation of small drops; *gut* as a term of the stomach and lower digestive apparatus appears to derive from Old English and still earlier a proto-Germanic word for a stream or channel (hence also, *gutter*), however, etymologies overlap and intertwine as "guttle" (below) comes not from *gut* perhaps, but *guzzle*, which has its roots in the Old French *gossiller* (to vomit, alternately, *prattle*) and which derives from *gosile*, for throat—not uncoincidentally a sort of carnal channel itself, which widens along the way to become the gut. And now even I am confused.

gurgulio (n) from Latin = gullet, obs.—meaning, well, the gullet. Extended to mean "appetite for food," as in Randolph (1630): "his palate is lost, and with it his gurgulio." Nature abhors a vacuum, after all.

gutling (n)—"a great eater; a glutton." obs, exc. dial., says the *Oxford English Dictionary* (hereafter *OED*), which I originally took to mean "obsolete and exceedingly dialect," but in fact means "obsolete, except in dialect," although they do not specify which dialects or of whence.

guttle (n)—The stuff of gluttony, which is to say, what one consumes gluttonously. It derives, interestingly, from the use of *gut* as a verb meaning not to eviscerate or "de-gut," as in (modern) common parlance, but rather to stuff oneself. You know, really muscle one's guts around with foodstuffs. Hence *guttle* also as a verb, for which we have "to eat voraciously; to gormandize." I have elsewhere (see *Food and Trembling*, 2011) gotten into Walter Benjamin's use of *go(u)rmandize* that is so out of keeping with either the Gastronomic Hierarchy (in descending order of refinement: gastronome, gourmet, friand, gourmand, goulu, goinfre), or Brillat-Savarin's definition, elaborated in *The Physiology of Taste, or, Meditations on Transcendental Gastronomy* (1825). Without revisiting all that here, it suffices to note that the *OED*'s use of *gormandize* is controversial. Although, how controversial really depends on who you ask and whether or not they've been dead for 150 years.

guttable (adj)—"that may be 'gutted,' or guzzled." Or, I should think, guttled? The strange thing is the *OED* only gives it as an adjective, but in the example provided, from Swift, it clearly operates as a noun or, more accurately, a nominalized adjective: "I have plenty of guttables; if we had agreeable companions as plenty as woodcocks, ducks, snipes...this would be a paradise" (1735). Slippery stuff, English. There is something very nice about the sentiment in Swift—like, "Oh, we have so much delicious food, now if only we had people to eat it with who were as enjoyable company as the food is fare, everything would be just perfect." It defies the greed implied by many of the other terms that constellate around the idea of gluttony, appealing to the notion that the appreciation of great food invites not only voracity but also good company, that the bounty lies not only in the quantity but the sharing thereof.

To say nothing of *gorge, gnaw, glut, gulp,* and so forth.
Meaning weaves and reels, and we with it.

---

1 Frederick Dedekind, *Grobianus et Grobiana,* 1739, translated by Roger Bull.

On Bad Melons, Bullshit, and the Emergent Qualities of Wine

i. The Click of the Latch

> Though some degree of knowledge develops from this passion, it never quite hardens into certainty. It remains, instead, something against which to continually test one's faculties and one's desire to apprehend the realities of another, fluctuating and intangible world—that of aromas, tastes, balances and harmonies. A fragile world, for which those of an artistic sensibility always feel a certain nostalgia, which expresses itself subtly, discretely and almost shyly through matter. —Nicolas Joly[1]

Big talk for a bunch of smashed-up fruit, one might say. Or another, one like me, might say, "Yeah Nicky, tell it. Tell me about it." I've written often about the perplex of taste, those instances of uncertainty and engagement, even provocation, when what is happening in our mouths calls more insistently upon our faculties than to simply decide whether we do or do not like the taste.[2] Or when we are pretty sure that we do, but are not sure why. And sure I've had this with scotch and chips and chocolate bars and the occasional lung or other stinking junk, but for me nowhere is this more vividly elaborated than in wine.

I cannot presume to universalize, but I believe this momentary confusion is the point of entry for many of us; at least, I have seen it written on the faces of so many people for whom I have poured wine and with whom I have shared wine. I have talked a lot of shit in the past on the shopworn cliché of the singular experience upon which one's subsequent life as a culinary devout turns—the Platonic strawberry, granny's cookie dough, an oyster off the Breton coast—so I am loath to step headlong into that literary trap, but here it is: I remember the wine I was drinking when I first felt that click. It was on my thirtieth birthday, for I am a late bloomer, having only started to drink in earnest at the age of twenty-two, after a long stretch of somewhat conflict-ed if exultant straightedge mayhem and misadventure, and with discernment considerably later. Out for dinner, I asked our sommelier what he would recommend for our meal, or, I added, whether there was anything he was excited about. At this his eyes lit up, and he returned with two bottles in hand. One would make a fine accompaniment for our meal and carry us through the appetizers into our first course, he explained; the other was what he was excited about. It likely would not make for a perfect meal pairing, but it was something a little interesting, a little different. Of course we chose the latter.

I'm not going to pretend that I remember exactly how it tasted, or that I was immediately transported, but I do remember it took me off guard, and that it tasted unlike any other wine I had tasted before; indeed, that I did not know wine could taste like.[3] And that was the click—not so much the sound of a final piece falling into place, but like the click of a latch being undone, a door coming just ajar, and the opening up of a space of possibility. I had already for some time been trying to figure out my way into wine: I knew there must be something out there beyond depan-neur wine, that justified paying more than dep prices, but it remained elusive. I started a sort of wine club with a pair of similarly curious friends, to taste bottles in a communal and somewhat systematic fashion and to try to get our heads around the phenomenon (I had read Terry Theise's *Reading between the Wines*, and he said you had to have a system). We fumbled through, and the wines tasted better than dep wines, but they still just tasted like...wine. This bottle tasted like something different. Still wine, but also like things other than wine, excitingly, confusingly other.

This is what I sometimes see on people's faces, the shock of (mis)recognition that adds another layer or dimension to the (also very essential) experiences of slaking one's thirst, washing down a meal, or getting roaringly, ecstatically drunk. I might say that it is the shock of drinking and tasting suddenly becoming interesting, whether or not one ends up pursuing these initial impressions and attempts to parse or make further sense of them. But some of us do.

ii. Varieties of Bullshit

The question of taste in wine—and still more of quality—is a fraught one. In fact, the big question one often hears is "Isn't it all bullshit anyway?" My response varies from a sustained "Ennnhhhhhhhh...kind of?" to a more judicious "Well, it depends on what you mean by that." I understand the motivation—rich people are annoying and we are right to begrudge them their pleasures. Wine seems an especially worthy target because it comes already steeped in class distinction, particularly (although this is changing) in Canada and the United States, where it is less embedded in the workaday culinary and drinking culture than in many European countries. And even as wine drinking has become more common in North America, "fine wine" predictably retains an aura of elitism. There is also a lot of other bullshit. Bordeaux futures are bullshit. The mobilization of bucolic peasant iconography by multinational beverage concerns is bullshit. The institution and economy of wine rating is bullshit. That said, I also think a lot of the rhetoric of "calling bullshit" on wine is itself bullshit.

Robert Parker, the founder of *Wine Advocate* magazine and quite possibly the most influential opinion-maker in the industry, has reputedly insured his nose and palate for $1 million. A high-scoring Parker review can mean literally millions in revenue to a winemaker, potentially doubling or even tripling the market price of a bottle.[4] Parker originally developed his 100-point rating scale in part as a counterpoint to what he perceived as the elitist and obscurantist frippery of mid-century French and British wine writers. He is styled as a straight-shooting type of guy, certainly not an aesthete (for that's the last sort we want weighing in on our sensual and aesthetic pleasures, right?), but "an ordinary American, a burly, awkward, hardworking guy from the backcountry of northern Maryland, about half a step removed from the farm."[5] Although Parker conceived his mission as cutting through "the bullshit"—in this case, the elaborate pretenses of a far-too-rich-seeming descriptive discourse that offered the average wine-drinker more literary allusion than any sense of what they could expect the stuff to actually taste like—he has become very much a part of the wine establishment, and similarly has suffered his own share of criticism for contributing to the weight of the bullshit in the wine world. Supplementing his 100-point scoring system, Parker has his own descriptive lexicon—be it "marzipan, minerals, stones, earth, and toasted hazelnuts" or the relative muscularity or femininity of a bottle of wine, and it is as much this notion that wine can give rise to such diverse sensory impressions as that it is amenable to a numerical rating system, that many take issue with.

In recent years, we have seen a number of studies and experiments trotted out that supposedly confirm wine tasting is bullshit. That the ratings by so-called wine experts vary widely between tasters and tastings, that experts are incapable of telling fine wine from plonk, or red from white, or even that two glasses are in fact from the same bottle of wine, poured twice in the same blind tasting, vindicate us in our suspicion that it is all but artifice and empty pageantry.[6] But when UK science journalist David Derbyshire triumphantly proclaims that wine tasting is "junk science," he makes an obvious sort of category mistake; because of course wine tasting is, well, not science. Appreciation of a particular wine varies widely between tasters? Of course it does. Preconceptions about price and prestige attached to a bottle encourage tasters to look for virtue rather than fault, and interpret challenging tastes accordingly? *Quel surprise!* Tasters can't tell white wine from red in the dark? Maybe we should take this as an opportunity to think about the limitations of our presuppositions about what distinguishes red from white wine.[7] Anyone—expert, consumer, journalist, Internet troll, or otherwise—who thinks there is a static, universal measure of wine goodness, and that they are Woodward & Bernstein-ing their way to the Great Debunk when they reveal the inconsistency and susceptibility to external influence of experts, is missing the point. I don't mean that the wine industry is not perverse and decadent and corrupt, because, you know, obviously it is. And I don't just mean that all taste is "personal" (sure it is, who cares); I mean that you can crow about how unscientific and therefore bogus wine tasting is and how everyone is just deluding themselves into deriving a diversity of pleasures from drinking the stuff, while you sit in your man cave eating bread crusts soaked in tap water and warm Pabst, or you can take that indeterminacy, that uncertainty, as a productive force and a point of departure. Is wine tasting bullshit? Sure, to the extent that art and music and feelings and all the creative endeavours of human existence are bullshit, and that, ultimately, existence itself is bullshit.

iii. Orthodoxies of Taste

Short of the fantasy of a universal, absolute "measure of all (wine) things," there nevertheless remains a well-established infrastructure of knowledge, norms, and expectations that serve to organize experience in wine. Knowledge of grape varieties, wine-growing practices, and winemaking traditions, familiarity with the baroque and ever-expanding appellation system that confers identity on a specific wine from a specific place, is all stuff that is rather esoteric and somewhat intimidating for the casual wine drinker. I do believe that it can enrich appreciation by allowing one to make connections previously unavailable (like how one's appreciation of any given episode of *The Simpsons* is enriched by a familiarity with, say, the entire history of American film), but as any good Foucauldian or deconstructivist dickbag is aware, such epistemic scaffolding is by its nature both enabling and constraining. This passage from Harold McGee has particular resonance for this discussion:

> It reminds me of a conversation I once had with Jeffrey Steingarten about a melon I'd tasted. It was wonderful, I told him, and really interesting because there was a hint of the squash family to its taste, a pumpkin-y note. (Melons and cucumbers and squashes are all in the

same family.) Jeff said, "So what you're saying is that it was a bad melon, McGee. Have you never heard of connoisseurship?"[8]

Arguably, the bone that so many (myself, to a certain extent) have to pick with wine tasting as an institution is that a collection of subjective experiences are being passed off as objective assessments, which ultimately have considerable prescriptive power: this is what fine wine is, this is what it should taste and smell like, this is why or how you should or should not like it. Steingarten calls it connoisseurship; I think about this in terms of "orthodoxies of taste," i.e., the "right way" of knowing subjective experience of external stimuli. I don't want to come down too hard against some aspect of prescriptivism in wine—the notion of typicity (how a wine made from x grapes in x part of x region should taste, given what we know about the foregoing and all it entails) is very helpful, and necessarily has a normative dimension—but there is a foreclosure, a constraining of avenues for appreciation, that I find troubling. Was McGee's melon bad because it suggested something of its squashy *confrères*? This holds only if what constitutes a good melon entails the total exclusion of any such reminiscences, and, in that case, according to whom?

The analogy is most salient in the case of so-called natural wine. I don't want to spend too many words on what that phrase means, for it has proven controversial in its own right, but some background is necessary to situate the present conversation. Taking its cue from the work of scientist and oenologue Jules Chauvet, who studied processes of fermentation and advocated for winemaking that eschewed selected yeasts and use of sulphur dioxide (an antimicrobial, stabilizer, and preservative commonly used in winemaking) as much as possible, what has become the natural or naturalist wine movement evolved from Chauvet's teachings into something beyond method—a philosophy, even an ethos of minimal intervention in winemaking. While "minimal intervention" could itself mean many things, the basic idea is to farm with minimal or no use of pesticides to encourage biodiversity and soil health in the vineyard, rely only on indigenous yeasts for fermentation, and avoid any chemical additives to correct or manage such factors as sugar, alcohol, or acidity in the wine. Nothing added, nothing taken away, is how it is often expressed. Some do more (by which I mean less); some do less (by which I mean more). Natural wine, unlike organic or even biodynamic, is not a regulatory label or certification, but a loose assemblage of idea(l)s and practices. "Despite the difficulty of pinning down the exact meaning of natural," write Goode and Harrop, "the category genuinely exists."[9]

One of the consequences (or aims) of this approach is what is conceived as a truer expression of not only the grapes or the terroir (that ambiguous and heterogeneous complex of fruit and vine and soil and microflora and human curation), but of the material agency of the wine itself. What this can sometimes mean is the occurrence of tastes and smells that may fall outside of the spectrum of acceptability for wine from a given place, or even wine tout court, depending on whose definitions one abides. "Farmy" aromas of wet hay, trampled autumn leaves, or manure might be interpreted variously as signs of spoilage, of healthy microbial diversity, or of a lack of oxygen in the winemaking or bottling process. Opacity in the glass is according to many standards a flaw, but may also be an intentional decision to prolong the effect of lees contact or avoid a merely cosmetic intervention. A bracing, driving acidity might be experienced as unpleasantly sour by a palate attuned to rounder, sweeter, fuller-bodied wines. Without getting lost in a quagmire of organoleptic and technical details, the point is that sometimes natural wines taste weird.

But more than that, natural wine is not content to taste "weird" within a register of taste and tastes established and maintained by what natural winemakers (and drinkers) see as the conventional (or, more pejoratively, industrial) wine world. Rather, natural wine (sometimes) embodies a critique of those orthodoxies of taste, insisting in part on a historicization of the standards and practices that parse diversity into varying degrees of acceptability and pathology—they point to the current standards of taste as effects of and aesthetic justifications for the encroachment of agribusiness rationality and blind progressivist mentality into wine, displacing previous tastes and practices. It is not quite the case that all wine's faults are now reborn as virtues (although, the antinatural backlash sometimes proclaims it so), but there has certainly been an attempt to reclaim and reinterpret the oenological abject in light of different aesthetic, quasi-ethical priorities, which back seat the "modern" emphasis on producing a predictable, consistent consumer product tailored to particular markets.[10] And they can be wonderful, really interesting, those bad melons.

iv. Fumbling toward Objectivity

Historian-sociologist of science Steven Shapin, best known (if known at all) for his influential work with Simon Schaffer, *Leviathan and the Air-Pump*, about scientific experimentation, fact-making, and social order in the crucible of the seventeenth century, has also written extensively on the history of wine and wine tasting as a means of exploring "public contests about the boundaries between what is subjective and what is objective, about where objectivity can and cannot go, and about how it is intelligible and right to talk about subjective experiences."[11] He charts how the ways people have talked about wine have changed considerably across time and place, from a concern with the health and constitutional properties of wine within Galenic humoral medicine, through a high purple prose and literary allusion of the nineteenth and early twentieth centuries, to the referential and at times molecularly informed lexicon of the present day:

> Medicine has become far less important in talking about wine, while the chemical sciences involved in identifying constituents in natural products have come to stand in an ultimately causal, but edgy, relation with the subjective experiences of taste and smell. Finally, the social changes which altered the place and function of wine drinking in many cultures spawned new vocabularies of taste, partly meant to parse the sensory effects of wine in a culture increasingly wanting to know what things were made of and what things were worth and increasingly skeptical of evocative vocabularies which were associated with an aristocratic, and possibly corrupt, old social order.[12]

The emergence of a highly referential language for describing wine (x wine smells or tastes of cedar, plums, leather, and tobacco) in lieu of an allusive, associative approach ("You do not feel it quarrelling with your liver—no, it is rather a Peacemaker, and lies as quiet as it did in the grape...the more ethereal Part of it mounts into the brain, not assaulting the cerebral apartments like a bully in a bad-house looking for his trull and hurrying from door to door bouncing against the wainstcoat, but rather walks like Aladdin about his own enchanted palace so gently that you do not feel his step"—mind you, this is coming from John Keats rather than your run-of-the-mill wine critic[13]) in some ways progressed apace, or slightly ahead of scientific inquiry into the chemistry of olfaction and gustation (smell and taste). This analytic mode of wine tasting really came into the fore in the 1970s, in large part through the work of Maynard Amerine and Edward Roessler in the UC Davis Department of Viticulture and Enology. Amerine and Roessler explored and developed experimental conditions that best allowed them to strip away or otherwise protect against the intrusion of highly subjective or situational factors that would contaminate an individual's assessment of what a wine really tasted like, along with statistical techniques to account for variability across different tasters' evaluations. Effectively, they were trying to develop an apparatus by which a collection of subjectivities could be transformed into objectivity, to "[render] private taste sensations into reliable and stable facts about objects in the world."[14]

The project was further refined by their colleague, Ann C. Noble, who developed the Wine Aroma Wheel that is now widely reproduced in texts and courses on wine connoisseurship. The wheel presents flavour groupings in a series of concentric circles of increasing specificity as one moves out from the centre. For example, in the middle you find earthy, woody, floral, fruity, et cetera; moving outward we might get fruity > tree fruit > peach; or herbaceous/vegetative > canned (vs. fresh) > canned asparagus. While such a rarified and technical object can quite understandably be seen as a plaything for nerds and fops, it was intentionally designed to provide a shared, standardized set of references to facilitate communication between producers, industry intermediaries, and consumers. Shapin has referred to the wheel as a "homespun intersubjectivity engine," arguably a sort of technology aiming at the democratization of taste by providing a shared language that is more or less grasp-able by any user.

Attempts at democratization and consensus are often in tension with concerns about what is ostensibly "right" and "true," or, in the case of wine, what is "really there." Get-ting everyone to agree on what canned asparagus smells like, and that this aroma is present in x wine is one thing, but the quest for a more robust objectivity has long turned on the priority of molecular-chemical accounts. Much of formal wine tasting (and increasingly, of especially nerdy amateur enthusiast tasting) has come to incorporate such accounts as they have been made available by oenological science. The appearance of green-pepper aromas in some Cabernet Francs and Sauvignon Blancs (and in green pep-pers themselves) has been attributed to concentrations of the compound 2-methoxy-3-isobutylpyrazine; the petrol nose of some Rieslings to 1,1,6-trimethyl-1,2-dihydro-naphthalene; the spicy character of Syrah to the phenolic ketone zingerone; and vanilla aromas to the more easily remembered compound vanillin (a.k.a. 4-hydroxy-3-me-thoxybenzaldehyde). And although wine talk is far from being colonized by such chemical-reductionist discourse, it has become less unusual for wine dorks to talk about terpenes, esters, and thiols, or the role of the yeast brett-anomyces in imparting pleasant (bacon, black cardamom) or less pleasant (used Band-Aid, horse saddle, horse shit) notes.[15] The Aroma Wheel embodies some of this lexical tension, in several places listing familiar flavours alongside chemical accounts—skunk and garlic alongside mercaptan and hydrogen sulfide, linalool amidst the roses and orange blossoms, or the befuddling trajectory of "fruity > other > methyl anthranilate (foxy)."

At a certain point, however, such molecular-chemical accounts tend to hit a wall, for as flavour scientists are ready to admit, a great number of widely recognizable aromas and tastes remain opaque or recalcitrant to chemical explanation. I am hesitant to cast such approaches as "reductionist," because while they attempt to break phenomena down into ever smaller components, at the same time they often result in the proliferation of new kinds of complexity—far from determining a single origin or explanation for a wine's flavour, we have instead an explosion, a multiplication of ways of understanding, not all of them commensurable. As is often the case, if one follows the science and the scientists far enough down the rabbit hole, instead of getting to the bottom of things, one comes out the other side of reductionism, into, as it were, a terrain of irreduction, where the neat compartmentalization of elements and influences no longer holds.[16] Beyond even our ability or inability to eventually isolate and identify all the chemical components of wine, there remains the question of where this ultimately gets us. James Hutchinson, a synthetic organic chemist with the UK's Royal Society of Chemistry, is quoted to this effect in Derbyshire's "Wine-tasting: It's Junk Science" article, which is somewhat strange to me, as his testimony seems to contribute to a sense of the possibilities of tasting, rather than take away from it:

> In terms of replicating what a human can do we are a long way off [...] The one thing we can do well, though, is a lot of amazing analytical chemistry that allows us to detect a huge range of different compounds in a

glass of wine. We can start to have an indication of how the acidity balances with the sweetness and different levels of flavour compounds. But the step we haven't got to is how that raw chemical information can be crunched together and converted into something that reflects someone's emotional response. That might be something we can never achieve.[17]

v. Poetic Materialism?

An analytic, molecular-chemical approach to taste can be extremely interesting and informative, but I am not convinced—rather, I am wary of accepting—that it constitutes the underlying reality of wine, the objective base or raw material upon which our subjective impressions and interpretations may be overlaid. There is another approach to tasting wine that I want to posit alongside this analytic mode, one that is more exploratory than arbitrative, more a wilful syncretism than an analytic accounting. It rubs up against the orthodoxies of taste but neither fully rejects nor fully falls within them. I have my own problems with the analytic impulse, as should by now be abundantly obvious. My inclination is always to break things down, take things apart, rather than to accept them as they are, take them at face value. It is not necessarily something I am proud of. Although, even that is not entirely true: I am proud of it—it seems to me not only a valuable skill, but something approaching a virtue in itself, and I do not think I would be wildly exaggerating to say that it has served—intentionally or not—as one of the organizing principles of my life. It can also be terribly incapacitating and violent, both internally and externally, as everyone from Derrida to Donna Haraway to anyone who has ever had to sit in a classroom with your average philosophy bro can attest. Thus, maintaining a sort of radical skepticism about the value and the limitations of analytic modes for knowledge, understanding, and appreciation has come to play an increasingly important, hopefully not antagonistic role in my relation to, and my relations in, the world. I try to temper my inclination to decompose a thing in order to figure it out, with the resolve that understanding may derive equally from the experience itself as from the examination of the experience. I suppose I'm not talking about wine anymore.

But I am still talking about wine. And in this sense I would say that wine tasting is as much a synthetic practice as it is an analytic one. Not merely the taking apart of a complex whole to reduce it to its simple components, but the drawing together of heterogeneous elements—the immediate sensory impressions, the tastes and smells of the wine, memory and expectation, wild association and the influences of book learning or bottles tasted, one's already underlying affect, the thrill of the body at the prospect of drunkenness or the enjoyment of that prospect realized, the pleasure of pleasures shared—in order to understand them as a relational whole, and experience them as something different, something irreducible, nothing less than the complex of experience coming to bear on the tasting itself. Something that is in fact a creative process, actively engaging us in the imaginative work of experience. On the challenges of defining and reproducing tastes, Raffi Khatchadourian writes:

> Flavor is a cognitive figment. The brain fuses into a single experience the results of different stimuli registered by the tongue, nose, eyes, and ears, in addition to memories of previously consumed meals. For rea-

Jonah Campbell

sons that are not fully understood, we perceive flavor as occurring in our mouths, and that illusion is nearly unshakable, as is made clear by our difficulty identifying, with any reasonable specificity, the way each of our various senses contributes to the experience.[18]

Here I would like to return to the Nicolas Joly quote with which I opened. Joly is a French winemaker from the Loire and one of the most influential proponents of biodynamic winemaking, an approach to agriculture derived from the teachings of the turn-of-the century Austrian philosopher/ecologist/spiritualist/nutjob Rudolf Steiner, who in turn was heavily influenced by the anti-Newtonian scientific writings of Goethe, which, it occurs to me only now, dovetails rather nicely with both the debates over experimental method discussed in Shapin and Shaffer's aforementioned *Leviathan and the Air-Pump*, and the very claims about irreduction and relationality that I am apparently making right now. Anyway, when Joly isn't busy making world-renowned Chenin Blanc or burying horns filled with ground quartz and spraying his fields with dandelion flowers fermented in cow mesentery, he also writes very beautifully and intuitively about wine. Of the uncertain and ever contingent knowledge-passion some feel about wine, he writes: "It remains, instead, something against which to continually test one's faculties and one's desire to apprehend the realities of another, fluctuating and intangible world." In this way we might speak of the poetic dimension of wine, not in the conventional sense of employing flowery, descriptive language (although that, too), but in terms of the original philosophical sense of poeisis as a bringing-forth or coming-into-being, the production or emergence of form, the transformation of the not-yet into the actual. I would also happily cut Joly off halfway, mid-

212

sentence where my reading mind always comes to rest in this passage, with "one's desire to apprehend the realities of another." For as much as I cherish drinking alone, bellied up to whatever bar will have me, a great part of the pleasure of wine tasting is that exchange and communication, coming together not as authorities, or experts in one-upmanship, or as scientific adepts bent on discovering or deciding, objectively, how a wine "really" is, but as messy, idiosyncratic, enthusiastic chumps attempting to fumble our way out of the darkness and isolation of individual subjectivity, and intersubjectively explore the emergent qualities of that wine, in that moment, in that place. The lexicon is necessarily mixed, then, for there is a real of the wine that may be expressed in terms of its chemical composition, of what elements inhere in the wine, but there is also a real that is expressed in the taste of "watered-down blood and the whites of strawberries," or in an impression of crystalline structure, or, as Evelyn Waugh once wrote, in the "elegant and malicious" character of a wine. The taste lasts as long as the wine, and then is gone—but the traces are not forgotten, for as my friend Craig is so fond of saying, "The more you taste, the more you taste."

In the end, what I am trying to get at with the "shock of (mis)recognition" is that it may just be easier (and more fruitful) to understand a wine if we do not from the outset assume that the subject/object distinction holds. The shock of a good wine is the realization of how much work is required to produce and maintain that separation of worlds—body and mind, flesh and spirit, the brute chemical material of the wine on one hand and our interpretation of it on the other—and what potential understandings may arise if we abandon the work of being that ontological cop. At my most foolhardy, pretentious, and romantic, I have often entertained the notion that through wine, through this provocative muddling of sensation and subjectivity, I might find a way out of the endless reflexivity of the analytic mode and back to my body, which has through years of negation, intentional rejection, and unexplained illness come to feel as much an opaque, unknowable antagonist— the ol' hell of the flesh—as the very condition and literal incarnation of my existence. I mean, I probably won't, but I do like the taste.

Appropriately, it turns out that there is even some endorsement of this inclination (or at least a poetic irony) in the etymology of the word *analysis* itself: while in conventional usage, the word has only ever really meant to break things down, take things apart, its Greek root *analyein* means to "unloose, release, set free; to loose a ship from its moorings." Free, seemingly, of the destructive implications that currently attend analysis, and of the naive holism of synthesis, but retaining the sense of opening up a space of possibility. I am condoned, if accidentally, by Aristotle, and so I continue looking, listening, waiting, for the click of the latch.

---

1 *Biodynamic Wine Demystified* (Board and Bench Publishing, 2008), 2.

2 Note: Technically, what I am writing about here is not just taste, but that complex of taste and smell that falls under the heading "flavour." My choice to continue to use the word *taste* throughout this section is both stylistically and conceptually motivated. In the first place, *flavour* feels to me a sort of tepid word, and I don't want to have to write it a hundred times. Second, although in wine speak "taste" and "aroma" are supposed to belong to the senses of taste and smell, respectively, this is

already somewhat of a fudging, since much of what is considered under taste is partly a product of our sense of touch (tannins, impressions of weightiness or fluidity influenced by the alcohol or acid content of the wine), and, for that matter, of our sense of smell, because retronasal olfaction is a major part of our experience of how things taste in our mouths. Mind you, there is danger in not attending to how so much of wine's complexity derives from the difference between, and interplay of, smell and taste—wines that smell wildly different than they taste being a wellspring of excitement—but I am going to stick to my guns and continue my loose and generalized use of *taste*. Taste is always already touch and smell, and *flavour* is too flat a word, and hell, it originally just means "smell" anyway (look it up, it's actually true).

3 The bottle in question was a Dinavolino of uncertain vintage, from Giulio Armani in Emilia-Romagna. I have had it many times since, and it remains a favourite.

4 Steven Shapin, "Hedonistic Fruit Bombs," *London Review of Books*, vol. 27, no. 3., 2005.

5 William Langwiesche, "The Million Dollar Nose," *Atlantic*, December 2000.

6 A couple of typical articles in the "bullshit" vein are: David Derbyshire, "Wine-tasting: It's Junk Science," *Observer*, June 23, 2013; and Robbie Gonzalez, "Wine Tasting Is Bullshit. Here's Why," Gizmodo (blog), May 8, 2014. The topic has of course been explored in more nuance as well, for example, by Calvin Trillin in "The Red and the White," *New Yorker*, August 19, 2002.

7 Not to sound like a dick, but some of the most interesting wines I have had troubled just this dichotomy: a Portuguese Bairrada wine made almost completely from the white grape Fernão Pires, with a mere 6 percent of the red Baga grape, that poured a deep, confounding red in the glass; the diaphanous Corail red wines of the Jura that defy even the intermediary category of rosé; or the skin-macerated "amber" wines of Georgia and Friuli-Venezia Giulia that, while still technically white, can grip the inside of your mouth like a leather glove steeped in tea.

8 Harold McGee, "The Science of Stale Coffee," *Lucky Peach*, issue 17, November 2015.

9 For a detailed, readable, and refreshingly non partisan discussion of natural wine, see Jamie Goode and Sam Harrop's *Authentic Wine: Toward Natural and Sustainable Winemaking* (University of California Press, 2013).

10 I realize I keep alluding to this ethical dimension without really elaborating. The more polemical language of "natural," "real," "honest," "authentic," et cetera notwithstanding, one encounters time and again the notion that winemakers feel an almost moral obligation to give microbial and terroir factors freer rein in the winemaking process. This folds easily into an ideology of purity not dissimilar to primitivist and other nature-fetishizing streams of thought, but one may also read in it something of a Latourian acknowledgement of and consideration for non-human agency. For an extended discussion and ethnographic exploration of this topic, see Anna Krzywoszynska, *We Produce Under This Sky: Making Organic Wine in a Material World* (PhD Dissertation, University of Sheffield, 2012). "It is in moments of withdrawal, of refusing to kill yeast even when its activity may result in economically negative outcomes," Krzywoszynska writes, "that organic wine producers recognise yeast as an entity with its own *telos*, and thus give it an ethical value as 'an end in itself'."

11 "Tastes of Wine," *Rivista di Estetica* 51(1) 2012, 53.

12 "Tastes of Wine," 86.

13 "Tastes of Wine," 71.

14 See Steven Shapin, "A Taste of Science: Making the Subjective Objective in the California Wine World," *Social Studies of Science* 46(3), 2016; and Christopher J. Phillips, "The Taste Machine: Sense, Subjectivity, and Statistics in the California Wine World," *Social Studies of Science* 46(3), 2016.

15 A company called Arux even sells "Certified Wine Flavour Standards" in the form of capsules that may be added to a glass of water to provide an

objective taste and aroma reference. Their line includes "30 positive wine flavours, off-flavours and taints, together with 32 'Discovery' flavours."

16 I'm playing a little fast and loose here with the notion of irreductions laid out in the second—more metaphysical—part of Latour's *The Pasteurization of France*. I think this is fine, however, because he plays a little fast and loose with the concept himself, saying typically Latourian things like "Nothing is, by itself, either reducible or irreducible to anything else." For me what is useful about this concept is that it can stand in for trying to understand things always in terms of something else, that something else being explanatory, or more true, or more real. It allows for the "real" to be multiple and interactive, rather than singular and authoritative. You can reduce taste to molecules, but when you get there, you just end up with molecules, not with taste per se.

17 in "Wine-tasting: It's Junk Science."

18 "The Taste Makers," *New Yorker*, November 23, 2009.

Haltingly into the Night

After months of roommates, friends, acquaintances, and other big strong men threatening to just up and eat the goddamn thing some night when I was out of town, I finally decided to open the comically oversized half-pound Reese's Peanut Butter Cup I received for Christmas, only to find that, lo and behold, it had gone kind of stale. At least, I think it's gone stale. It's hard to tell. I am basing my assessment on the crumbly, borderline chalkiness of the peanut butter, which I remember from a youth of expired Halloween mini-cups as an indication that a Reese's product is somewhat past due. However, it is altogether possible this is not a matter of staleness; the denser consistency could be an unfortunate necessity of the product itself, a structural precondition for the success of such a scaling up, like how you have to start building insects differently if you want to grow them to car-destroying proportions, gravity being what it is. Maybe it's necessary to alter the consistency of the filling if there is to be any hope of the chocolate frame retaining its shape. I suppose I can't know.

My attitude toward what I will call the Big Big Cup—to distinguish it from the less monstrous, standard Big Cup—had changed over time. Initially, I was waiting for just the right occasion to bust it out as a post-dinner-party flourish, but it occurred to me that, having inexplicably written so much about Reese's products in the past,[1] I owed it to myself and to my craft to approach this abomination with an appropriate measure of respect. I had to eat it all, by myself. Not a task to be taken lightly, because the thing is huge. One could pull a muscle. A half-pound may not sound like much, but if you consider that a regular Reese's cup weighs approximately twenty-one grams, and the regular Big Cup weighs forty-nine grams, then, at roughly two hundred and twenty-seven grams, the Big Big Cup is almost eleven times the size of a regular cup. That's a lot of cup.

Perhaps this outsized sense of the importance of the task inevitably sealed my fate. Big Big Cup was thus endowed with a glamour, daunting and preposterous. When would I be ready? *Could* I be ready? How hungry would I have to be? Who would survive, and what would be left of them? I wouldn't say I was afraid; that would be too dramatic. In fact, I was looking very much forward to the experience, come what may. I foresaw myself suffused and sickened, surely, but animated and inebriated also by the poetry of excess. I would write something, maybe the best something, about the Biggest Cup (probably not actually the biggest cups, but I'm already drunk on poetry by this point in my fantasy), before crapulence swung around to destroy me.

And so at home I bided my time. One can't rush such things. Though perhaps I should have—for now, halfway through the Biggest Cup, I am hardly inspired to go on, and do not know whether it is in the cup or myself I should be disappointed. Was it ever the giant I took it to be, or just some dusty, crumbling windmill? The first impression I had upon tearing the package was the familiar and not entirely pleasant scent of a chocolate Easter rabbit, the big foil-wrapped kind. I don't know whether it is simply the smell produced by too much chocolate in a confined space—if that is in fact a thing—or whether it has something to do with chocolate left to languish, but it quickly filled the room. I may as well be in the package with it, this infernal cup. Even in the midst of my confusion, I marvel at the heft of the thing. The thickness of the chocolate around the bevelled edges defies any notion that the cup could possibly be in proportion to its predecessor; again, probably a structural necessity. Reluctantly, I am forced to admit that no growth serum or biggification ray was employed in the production of the Biggest Cup—a marvel of engineering it must be, impressive in its design if not livable in its execution.

There is something appropriate about this anticlimax that appeals to my failure-loving aesthetic sense. It is appropriate in the way that waiting for the right moment to do something—with full idiomatic approval: Good Things Come to Those Who Wait, Fools Rush In, Patience Is a Virtue, and so on—so often results in the squandering or spoilage of that which one has so long anticipated. I could argue that there is a difference between putting off doing what one desperately wants to do, and waiting for precisely the right moment to do something that one does not yet feel prepared to approach, but such a distinction may be a coward's comfort that nevertheless leaves one gazing up into the darkness, eyes burning with anguish and anger. So, bummed as I am, I cannot help but feel underneath it all a *sense* of satisfaction at being robbed, as much by my own machinations as by the relentless march of time and the shelf life of even the most denatured of confections. Robbed not only of the prospect of triumph, or of the confrontation about which I had so fantasized, but even of the capacity to understand what it is I have before me: I have in effect robbed myself of the sense of the event by too thickly encumbering it with significance.

Funny that I am all too ready to embrace the soul-killing general lesson of "Don't look too forward to things, for you shall inevitably spoil them before you have the opportunity to be let down," whereas if the specific lesson here is "Don't think so hard about candy bars," I don't want to learn it.

---

1 See *Food and Trembling* (Invisible, 2011).

If I Swallow Something Evil

stomach (v.) to cherish indignation or bitterness. from L. stomachari—to be resentful, to be angry with. See also, Fr. s'estomaquer—to take offence.

I love, as I can imagine others loathing, the English language for just such ambiguities, inconsistencies, and transformations as this. To think that, above and beyond the familiar organ of digestion, *to stomach* once meant the retention and even enjoyment of one's (metaphorical) bile, but has come over time to mean variously "to brook, put up with, endure or tolerate," a "relish, inclination, desire (for something immaterial)," "an appetite or relish for food," and, as above, even to relish one's own ill-feeling. When I first stumbled upon these multiple meanings, they struck me as almost opposite to the conventional use of *stomach*, its negation suggesting not just an absence of positive desire, but the very limits of tolerance—the ability to keep something down, literally or figuratively. But I see now how the meanings interweave, playing with and off each other, suggestively yet uneasily. Tolerance becomes desire (or desire tolerance, in cynical romantic analogy); we come to cherish our foods as once we cherished our venom and our pride.

This brings to mind another confusing human achievement: the *amaro*, or bitter liqueur. We in North America are most familiar with a handful of aperatifs/aperativos and digestifs/digestivos, but almost every country has their own beloved take on the bitter, from Jägermeister and the Kräuterlikors of Germany, to the gentian liquors of France, to the Latvian Riga Black Balsam (which tastes distinctly of caramelized vegetable sugars, among other things). Many of these can be traced to the apothecarial legacies of witches, herbalists, and snake-oil salesmen, macerating plants and whatnot (I like to think there were actual snakes involved) in alcohol for their ostensibly curative properties. One such concoction that has been wildly popular both in spite and by virtue of its strange and aggressive flavour is Fernet-Branca, the taste of which has been variously likened to "black licorice-flavoured Listerine," "medicine, mint, and bitter mud," and "poison, with aspirin crushed up in it." It is, as you can imagine, an acquired taste.

Created in 1845 in Milan by Bernardino Branca, and marketed as "febrifuge, vermifuge, tonic, invigorating, warming and anti-choleric," a cure-all for everything from menstrual pains to hangovers, it became so firmly entrenched as medicine that it escaped suppression during Prohibition in America. A feat that seems all the more remarkable today, since up until the 1970s it contained, in addition to its 38 percent alcohol, an apparently not insignificant quantity of opiates. Fernet is now widely recognized as a, as it were, recreational libation, as opposed to a purely medicinal one, but it certainly still tastes like medicine, and similar products retain their ambiguous status in this respect. Zwack Unicum (a Hungarian bitter that in a movie about its life would be played by Jägermeister—sweeter and more palatable for mainstream audiences), for instance, is in some places still sold behind pharmacy counters rather than in liquor stores, evoking for the bitters fan the queer sense of pride of having defied the presupposition that no one could appreciate the stuff for its gustatory merits (and creating another strange parallel between the privileged, bearded cocktail revivalist and the Listerine-drinking hobo).

There is a Fernet-Branca advertisement from some time

in the interwar years that I have always loved. Designed in Art Deco style by Lucien-Achille Mauzan, it depicts a winged, scythe-wielding angel of death fleeing a rolling bottle of Fernet, with three figures following in its wake, and a slogan that proclaims, "Fernet-Branca Estomacal. Prolonga la Vida!" One of the figures has his head turned and arm outstretched behind him, in a gesture I assume is intended to beckon others to follow, but which, in its stylish abstraction I always read as him giving the finger, in a very "Run comrade, the old world is behind you!" sort of way. Are they chasing Death away or merely chasing death? It is strange to make of the acrid, acerbic, and unpleasant a virtue, although the strangeness is somewhat congealed into a tiresome pretense in this era of adventure eating and ubiquitous foodism.

Nevertheless, I like the stuff. I wouldn't go so far as to say I liked it before it was cool, but at least before it was quite so predictable to do so. In a self-serving mixture of metaphors, I'm willing to make the claim that goddamn bastards such as myself may cherish our bitterness both in itself and for the bile it calls forth, to better aid the digestion of what we can and must keep down, and stimulate the appetite for other pleasures. "Is not the lute that soothes your spirit," wrote Kahlil Gibran, "the very wood that was hollowed with knives?"[1] Or something like that?

---

1 *The Prophet* (Knopf, 1923) was a great favourite of mine back when I was a Sensitive Young Man, before I became so cold and spiritually feckless.

You're Not a Beauty, but Babe You're Alright

I have just exited the little Lebanese boulangerie/pizza place tucked beneath the stairs on that street downtown (only one of many) that seems to be eternally under construction. The shop still has its salad bar on the left, the case of baklava and other desserts to the right, tucked under the stairs I always forget actually lead somewhere, but these have all gone unheeded and I have ordered what I always order, a *za'atar tout garni* (or, as often, "za'atar all-dressed"). Because that is how one does at Al Taib, or any of the Al Taib outlets, whose number seems to fluctuate between two and five at any given time. It cost me $3.25, which is a 62.5 percent increase over the price when I first moved to Montreal. But, you know, even that ain't bad for a delicious sandwich. Once one accepts that the za'atar is no longer shockingly cheap, and makes peace with its entry into relative economic intelligibility within the culinary landscape of the downtown core (at the westernmost edge of the anachronistic, euphemistic Golden Square Mile), it should not be difficult to preserve one's original enjoyment of the food. Although, eating it today, I began to think about how it is distinctly not a perfect food. The convention when writing about a delicious and regionally specific sandwich, I am willing to claim, is to make much fuss about the perfect balance that is struck by its ingredients—the yielding but toothsome quality of the bread, the freshness of the vegetables, the resolving power of the condiment. The sandwich as a work of art.

Now, I love za'atar, but I have enough associations—emotional, biographical, (sub)cultural—to make for its romanticization without resorting to such hackneyed adulation. What we call in passing the za'atar is a man'ousheh or Levantine flatbread spread with za'atar spice, a mixture of thyme, sumac, olive oil, and sesame seeds, rolled with vegetables. The za'atar ordered *tout garni* gives you lettuce, tomatoes, black and green olives, onion, hot peppers, fresh mint, and pickled turnips, and is a creature a little in excess of itself, a briny, potentially overwhelming clamour of tastes. Consider how four out of the eight toppings are pickled or otherwise preserved, and how the sumac of the za'atar itself adds a further astringent note. That the remaining ingredients that actually taste like anything include raw onions and mint leaves (mint: essential) does not make for a delicate or well-integrated whole.

Rather, the za'atar is bright and bold and gripping, spicy and tart and bitter all at once, the earthier elements hardly serving to rein in the wilder proclivities of the other ingredients. And I am totally okay with this, because it is awesome. I could (and sometimes do) ask for tahini or garlic sauce or even a falafel ball for bulk, but there is a certain esoteric solemnity to ordering it *tout garni*—one of the first of the idiotismes Québécoises with which I learned to pepper my French speech in order to gradually appear perplexingly doltish and allophonic (I used to get asked if I was Russian a lot), rather than merely an Anglo. It was many years before I bothered to learn that the za'atar owes its name to the spice blend, and that the sandwich itself may be assembled in many ways.

There is a little falafel shop on the Trubarjeva cesta in Ljubljana, just a ways down the street from the famous Zmajski bridge that is adorned at each end with a pair of fearsome copper dragons. We were taken there because the food is good and cheap, and, we were told, there is a woman who works the counter with whom everyone falls in love. There,

I watched this woman make for me another kind of za'atar sandwich, so unlike that to which I had become accustomed: pita bread in lieu of manakish, dressed only with tomatoes and firm, salty, nigella-flecked nabulsi cheese, drizzled with olive oil, and only then dusted with za'atar. She had dark hair and pale, almost translucent skin; she probably loathed the fawning gazes of her clientele, and surely the dragons wagged their patinated tails when she crossed their bridge, but it was doomed to be, for me, an ersatz za'atar.

It is a comforting sandwich, the *tout garni*. And if ever I return to Montreal after a lengthy stint or a whole other life abroad to find all the Al Taibs shuttered and their particular take on the za'atar vanished, it will be with a more fully realized wistfulness that I look back on the summer nights and stoop-hangs of my early twenties, the beery 3:00 a.m. snackspeditions, and the warm, familiar heft of the za'atar, rolled up in its pink butcher paper. It is imbalanced, but it is imbalanced like we were imbalanced: a little too hot, a little too sour, a little too bitter. Manna for the emo-crusties. Everything louder than everything else. Forgive my sentimentality, I have a cold.

Afterword: A Note on the Title

In choosing a title for this book, I harboured some concern that *Eaten Back to Life* might suggest to the reader a sort of memoir of self-discovery and rejuvenation achieved via food. Taken this way, it could well conjure the romantic trope of a poor desperate soul—down in the dumps, over a barrel, suffering the mean reds—who, through adopting a culinary trade, eating healthy, or (god help them) starting a food blog, rediscovers their lust for life. This is the last impression I would hope to give, and the reader who embarked with any such expectations was, I regret, doomed from the outset to disappointment.

Eaten Back to Life is in fact a reference to the 1990 debut album of the Buffalo, New York, death-metal band Cannibal Corpse. I have no particular nostalgic connection to Cannibal Corpse (unlike, say, Bolt Thrower and their 1989 "World Eater," which was the first death-metal song I ever heard, tagged oddly enough onto the end of a Fugazi tape my brother dubbed for me, and also might have made for a passable book title), but the cover of the record depicts what is a probably freshly risen, living-dead type crazily devouring the hell out of itself (the undead need flesh to live, of course, although conventional wisdom goes that they tend to turn to the living for this purpose). The paradox is too inviting. The image and phrase together present a painting-oneself-into-a-corner type of situation, which suggests as its inevitable end result the creature reduced to an embarrassed, immobilized head and one-armed torso, who looks around after this frenzy of revitalizing, intoxicating autophagy and, realizing its predicament, thinks to itself, "Ah, nuts." Eating back to life, then, is of course always an eating-toward-death (*Essen-zum-Tode*, for you Heideggerians), driven and derided by taste.

A lot of mileage has been gotten out of the metaphoric potential of food for thinking about life, with greater or lesser degrees of profundity and success. But in the form of this hapless, heavy-metal ghoul we have a reminder that food, like life, is but another ever-twisting hole down which you descend, chasing some sense of satisfaction. You never truly reach the end; you just run out.

Acknowledgements

First and utmost, I must thank my mother, Mary. There often tends to be something of the cursory about acknowledgements, but I want to take this opportunity to reckon with my own rather typically male tendency to carry on as if I'd been born fully formed from the cloven head of Zeus, rather than made of, indebted to, formed, and informed by another human being. For while I suspect she views many of my gastronomic concerns as a touch trivial and portentous (how could she not—I am an absurd figure!), I see them as growing from a soil she prepared. Beyond the very real, too-often-unrecognized work of being a mother, cooking and caring for two kids and a husband (I have, in the past, in my own self-narrating failed to recognize, and have misrepresented, the primacy of this caregiving work, a testament to the self-serving contortions of memory), she always maintained a commitment to doing so in a way that felt meaningful on her own terms, engaging me as much as possible in that process. Whether growing a garden, keeping me around and underfoot in lieu of sending me to kindergarten, giving me a weekly night of responsibility to cook for the family, or just refusing to buy me Sugar Crisp, all of this contributed to a basic understanding that food *comes from somewhere*. Not just from a package, not simply from a store. Perhaps more importantly than the food itself, she imparted what I am inclined now to describe as a curiosity about the world, and a dissatisfaction with many of the *idées reçues* of the time, an unwillingness to accept the just-so stories that organized our lives. We have argued enough over the years, but I always recall on her part a willingness to explain and debate, rather than to merely invoke the parental authority of "Because I said so," even or especially when I was an entitled, petulant, teenage punk. This has certainly influenced my approach to food, and no less my approach to life itself. So, thanks.

For the matter more immediately at hand, a tremendous thank-you to John for being a patient, thoughtful, and incisive editor. There is likely no better motivator for an author than to have an editor one suspects may be a better writer than oneself. Thank you similarly to Leigh Nash for tolerating my endless rationalizations for seemingly arbitrary capitalization, and insisting that at least some of the time, some readers should be able to discern what the hell I am talking about. Thank you to Craig Schweickert for being an indispensable companion and guide in things oenological; Camilla Wynne for her friendship, chip-ship, and pastry counsel; Heather Vandenengel for her beer counsel; Nazlie Faridi for reining in my more outlandish and scientifically irresponsible speculations about neurology; Cheyanne Turions for pointing me to indigenous works on bannock and for any number of conversations about food, art, and politics; Gina Badger for helping me to understand cooking and eating as forms of love and struggle beyond the usual clichés; Katie Mathieu for being the first person to make me think about fermentation; and to Maddie Ritts for being the most game, indulgent, and combative dining partner I could hope for. Also to Barbara the cat for being a beacon to us all by refusing to entertain interest in any human food other than butter, and a beacon to me personally by being a little point of perplexing, loving light.

Parts of this text have appeared in some form on my blog *Still Crapulent After All These Years* (www.foodandtrembling.com), in the *National Post*, and elements of "The Cauldron of the Speckled Seas" appear in modified form in *en Route, April 2017*.

INVISIBLE PUBLISHING is a not-for-profit publishing company that produces contemporary works of fiction, creative non-fiction, and poetry. We publish material that's engaging, literary, current, and uniquely Canadian. We're small in scale, but we take our work, and our mission, seriously: our titles are culturally relevant, well written, beautifully designed, and affordable.

We are committed to publishing diverse voices and experiences. In acknowledging historical and systemic barriers, and the limits of our existing catalogue, we strongly encourage Indigenous and writers of colour to submit their work.

Invisible Publishing is also home to the Bibliophonic series, and the Snare and Throwback imprints.

If you'd like to know more, please get in touch:
info@invisiblepublishing.com

Invisible Publishing
Halifax & Picton